Potty Training

Lifesaving Techniques and Advice for an Easy Transition

Linda Sonna, Ph.D.

Adams Media
Avon Massachusetts

Published by Adams Media, an F + W Publications Company
57 Littlefield Street
Avon, MA 02322
www.adamsmedia.com

ISBN 10: 1-59869-331-6
ISBN 13: 978-1-59869-333-1

Printed in China.
J I H G F E D C B A

Library of Congress Cataloging-in-Publication Data
available from the publisher

This publication is designed to provide accurate and authoritative
information with regard to the subject matter covered. It is sold
with the understanding that the publisher is not engaged in render-
ing legal, accounting, or other professional advice. If legal advice
or other expert assistance is required, the services of a competent
professional person should be sought.
—From a *Declaration of Principles* jointly adopted by a
Committee of the American Bar Association and
a Committee of Publishers and Associations

Many of the designations used by manufacturers and sellers to
distinguish their product are claimed as trademarks. Where those
designations appear in this book and Adams Media was aware of
a trademark claim, the designations have been printed with initial
capital letters.

This book is available at quantity discounts for bulk purchases.
For information, please call 1-800-289-0963.

Mommy Rescue Guide

Welcome to the lifesaving *Mommy Rescue Guide* series! Each *Mommy Rescue Guide* offers techniques and advice written by recognized parenting authorities.

These engaging, informative books give you the help you need when you need it the most! The *Mommy Rescue Guides* are quick, issue-specific, and easy to carry anywhere and everywhere.

You can read one from cover to cover or just pick out the information you need for rapid relief! Whether you're in a bind or you have some time, these books will make being a mom painless and fun!

Being a good mom has never been easier!

Contents

Chapter 3: What Do We Need to Get Started? 53

Chapter 4: Is It Ever Too Early to Start Training? The Baby-Track Method 65

Chapter 5: How Can We Practice? Potty Practice Method 83

Introduction

MAKING THE SWITCH FROM diapers to underpants is a big transition! This milestone can be a fun, rewarding, and successful lesson as long as you, Mommy, do your research. That's why you picked up this book! Do you know that there are several different methods of potty training? Do you know that in order to pick the best method for you and your child, you should consider both of your personalities and the schedule in your household? Do you know how to baby-proof your bathroom? Do you know how to respond when your child has an accident or a potty success? You will know how to do these things and more after reading *Mommy Rescue Guide: Potty Training*.

Whether this is your first child or your fifth, each potty training experience will be different because each child is different. You can choose to read this book cover to cover, in order to plan for an easy transition or you can flip to the section you need when you have a specific question in mind! Either way, this book will help you make potty training easy, fun, and natural. This book takes the trauma out of this transition and makes a trip to the bathroom an exciting accomplishment.

Chapter 1

What's My Role?

MAYBE THIS IS YOUR first time as a potty trainer and you need to know how to begin. Knowing how to start can be daunting! Or, maybe this is not your first time, but you are looking for a method that works better for your situation. Every child is different. Before you start choosing methods, let's talk about what the job ahead entails for you and your family. Three things are key: patience, consistency, and compassion.

You, a Potty Coach

It's normal to feel nervous about potty training! Often, the very word "training" conjures images of housebreaking a pet. For this reason, many parenting experts want to eliminate the phrase "potty training" altogether. Instead, they speak of "potty learning." Whatever you call it, it is actually a quite straightforward process. As a coach, your jobs will be to work out a game plan and supervise practice sessions, as a teacher to provide instruction, and as a cheerleader to nurture a can-do attitude.

Your Role as Coach

Potty coaches should remember that little athletes need to be well rested, physically up to par, and emotionally ready to tackle a new skill. If your baby is ill, don't work on potty training until she is well. If your toddler is preoccupied with other problems, let her choose whether she wants to wear underpants and use the potty or go back to diapers. While wearing diapers she can practice other skills, such as checking from time to time to see if she needs a diaper change. That way, she continues to work on learning the difference between wet and dry.

Coaches recognize the importance of standing back and allowing children to struggle on their own. Too much hands-on help deprives children of the opportunity to learn. Too many verbal pointers distract them. On the other hand, coaches must not expect their young charges to do more than they can handle on their own. Otherwise, they become overwhelmed. Pointing out when your child needs to use the potty is likely to be very important until she is better at remembering on her own. Too few reminders can set her up to fail; too many can keep her from taking responsibility for herself. It's a matter of finding a balance.

Mindful Mommy

Compromise! If your toddler insists on wearing underpants when she has diarrhea or a bladder infection, try a waterproof diaper cover. That will lessen the mess and permit her to go to the potty by herself if she wishes.

Positive Practice

Coaches also know that when it comes to practice, more is not necessarily better. Conscientious toddlers may end up constantly worrying about having an accident. Too much concentration on toilet training can lead to burnout. Sometimes the best course is to put the whole subject out of both your minds for a time. There is more to life than potties!

Good coaches also try to ensure that each learning session ends on a positive note. Always express confidence that your child will learn in time. Pointing out how much he has mastered thus far prevents both of you from becoming discouraged.

Be Your Little One's Partner

Let's look at an example of a young mother and her son, Jenna and Tod. Like many of us mothers, Jenna was uncertain how to go about potty training her son. After talking to friends and relatives and reading some articles on the subject, she was sure her twenty-eight-month-old had sufficient bladder and bowel control to be trained, and since Tod disliked having

Mommy Must

If you assign a task that is too hard, such as using the potty, follow up with something easier, such as running to the potty, sitting down for two seconds, and jumping back up. Learning to get to the potty fast is important!

his diapers changed, he might gladly give them up. She took him to the store so he could help pick out a potty chair, bought a storybook on the subject, and purchased some stickers to use as rewards. Back at home, she promised that he could wear his new "big boy" underpants whenever he wanted to try the potty. Then she waited for Tod to signal interest. When a week went by and he still hadn't shown any interest, she decided it was time for a nudge.

Jenna read Tod the storybook again, and explained that he would soon use the potty just like the main character. It was summertime, so Jenna took off Tod's clothes and suggested he have some fun sprinkling the flowers out back. Then she explained that inside the house, he should go pee-pee in his little potty. After dinner that night he approached her and said, "Pee-pee." She walked him to the bathroom, helped him undress, and he urinated in the potty. "Way to go!" she exclaimed as she handed him a sticker and helped him don his "big boy" pants. She thought she was home clear—and she was!

Tod did have an occasional nighttime accident, and he had a two-week setback when his baby brother was born. But overall, Tod managed the potty like a

Mommy Must

Although it seems strange to many adults, a child must see himself eliminating to grasp that waste comes from his body. So, find a place where accidents won't do too much damage, and remove your child's diaper. When he begins relieving himself, point it out.

trooper. Jenna had a hard time relating to the troubles many of her friends recounted. It seemed to her that if children were physically ready, they would basically train themselves.

Be a Partner

Jenna did a lot of things right and her contribution to her son's training was far more important than she realized. First, she established that Tod had the wherewithal to control his bladder and bowel. Then she involved him in the process by letting him help choose a potty chair. She explained the procedures for using the potty by reading him a storybook. She offered the incentive of "big boy" pants and gave stickers as rewards. When she took off his diapers and let him urinate outside, she made sure he grasped the all-important concept that urine came from his body. Furthermore, Jenna didn't pressure Tod to perform. She gently praised his successes and didn't overreact when he had accidents. Sounds easy, doesn't it?

Problems Can Occur

Jenna discovered that some children find learning to use the potty a big challenge. When Jenna had a second child, she expected him to be even easier to potty train. Her youngest son, Jacob, idolized his big brother and liked to do whatever Tod did. By the time he was twenty months old, Jacob would occasionally follow Tod into the bathroom and urinate in the regular toilet alongside him. When Jenna was seven months pregnant with her third child, she wanted to get Jacob out of diapers before the next baby arrived. Unfortunately, things started to bog down almost immediately.

The Trained Parent

If Jenna caught Jacob at the right moment and took him to the toilet, he would use it. But try as she might, she couldn't get him to tell her when he needed to go. That meant several accidents each day. She tried incentives and rewards, storybooks and stickers, but nothing worked.

One day when Jenna heard Jacob grunting, she swooped him up despite his protests and ran him to the bathroom. He held it in until she let him get off the potty. A few minutes later, he messed in his pants. "You're supposed to go in the potty!" she said sharply. Jacob looked repentant, but the next time she tried to take him to the bathroom, he threw a tantrum. She ended up sending him to time-out, and he messed in his pants again.

Jenna tried to remain calm when Jacob refused to go near the potty over the next weeks, but she was

Mommy Must

Incentives such as regular underpants and the excitement of a new challenge can motivate children at the outset of potty training, but enthusiasm may later fade. Keep giving attention and encouragement until the habit of using the potty forms.

tired of diapers, and her advanced pregnancy was making her cranky. She began putting him on the potty at regular intervals, entertaining him by reading books and singing songs about potties. Sometimes he urinated while sitting on the potty. More often, he wet his pants shortly afterward.

Constipation became an increasingly serious problem. Jacob would go for days without having a bowel movement, then scream in pain when he tried. The pediatrician prescribed enemas and laxatives to relieve the hard, painful bowel movements. These remedies didn't cure the bigger problem. It got to the point that when Jenna so much as mentioned the potty, Jacob would cloak himself in silence. He refused to respond to her inquiries, explanations, and entreaties.

Jacob was still in diapers when he started kindergarten. If he was upset about being teased by his classmates, he kept his feelings to himself. The chronic soiling and frequent wetting continued.

Finally, Jenna determined that she had done everything in her power to help him. She placed the ball squarely in Jacob's court, trusting that sooner or later he'd pick it up and run with it. Six months later, he did!

Ending Power Struggles

Unfortunately, Jenna learned the hard way that when a parent and child end up in power struggles over the potty, the child wins every time, so everyone loses. The bottom line is that children's bodies are their own. Parents can't control when and where they eliminate.

Jacob's early potty successes had convinced Jenna that he was ready to be fully trained. But occasionally following a big brother into the bathroom for fun is one thing; going to the potty when there are other, more interesting things to do is quite another. Jacob might have been physically ready, but he wasn't able to handle so much responsibility.

Jacob's resistance hardened in the face of the pressure Jenna placed on him to perform. Soon he was in too much turmoil to hear the signals his own body was sending him, hazed as his mind was by anxiety. Even after his mother backed off, he needed time to heal emotionally before he could move forward.

It makes no sense to keep battling to get a car up a hill when the engine has stalled and you don't know what's wrong or how to fix it. If you lift the hood and begin pounding the engine with a hammer, you will do more harm than good. Pushing the car uphill requires a Herculean effort. In such a situation, you need to contain yourself and refrain from reacting until you can think clearly and decide how best to proceed. It's always possible to walk. Walking may even require less energy in the long run. In the case

Mindful Mommy

If you make mistakes during potty training, it may take your child a bit longer to learn, but your errors won't scar your child for life. The idea that potty training changes your child's personality is just plain wrong.

of potty training, that may mean putting the project on hold and returning to diapers for a month or two.

Saying the Right Things

Many of us wonder how to communicate with babies and toddlers who don't understand much of what we say and don't speak much, if at all. There are some special steps you can take to improve communication.

Show toddlers exactly what to do. Put a stuffed animal or a doll that wets on the potty. Enlist a willing sibling or parent to give a live demonstration. Read storybooks about potties.

Get your child's full attention before speaking. If you tell your child to go to the potty and get no response, she may not have even realized that you were speaking to her. Always begin by saying your child's name. Don't give instructions until she looks up.

Combine words with gestures. Point to the bathroom when you tell your child to go there. Pat the potty when telling him to sit down on it. Children understand more when you combine words with visual signals.

Tell your child what to do rather than what not to do. Sentences containing negative words such as "don't" are hard to grasp. To comprehend "don't stand up," children must understand "stand up," and then understand that "don't" means they are to do the opposite. That's too confusing! "Sit down" is much clearer.

Use consistent language. It's hard enough for a youngster to learn, "Go to the potty." He may not also understand, "Let Mommy take you to the bathroom," "Come with me to the potty," "Let's take you to the potty," "Let's get you to the toilet fast." Choose a single set of words and phrases, and try to stick to them.

Combine verbal instructions with manual guidance. Place your hands on your child's shoulders and apply gentle pressure while telling him to sit on the potty. Cover his hands with yours to help him remove his pants. Show him what to do while you tell him.

Combining verbal, visual, and physical direction helps children learn new vocabulary and enhances communication. To be a good teacher, use every means at your disposal to help your little student understand what he's supposed to do!

Providing Feedback

Potty training can be confusing to little ones. To coach effectively, you need to give your child lots of feedback to help him understand what is happening. There are three kinds of feedback.

1. Neutral feedback is a straightforward statement that gives youngsters information about what they are doing, for example, "You're

urinating." This kind of basic information is important for children who have always worn diapers and don't even realize when they are passing waste.

2. Positive feedback informs students about what they are doing correctly so they know to repeat it, for example, "Good! You're urinating in the potty!"

3. Negative feedback tells children what they are doing wrong, as in "Oh, no! You're urinating in your pants!" If you give negative feedback, be sure to tell your child how to correct the mistake: "Oh no! You're urinating in your pants! You need to do that in the potty!"

Some toddlers are bolder and more confident than others. They may not learn much from negative feedback but aren't especially daunted by it, either. Other children are far more sensitive. Even a hint that they are doing something wrong destroys their confidence, and they give up. They need lots of positive feedback! Recognize what type of feedback will most effectively help your little one.

Warm Fuzzies and Cold Pricklies

Let's see how these different types of feedback come into play. Say you instruct your child to sit on the potty and she stays there for only two seconds before jumping up. You have a choice about how you respond. You can give neutral feedback by describing exactly what she did, "You sat on the potty, and then you stood up." This can be helpful to children who are especially oppositional and seem to want to do the opposite of whatever you want them to do. You could give positive feedback to let your child know she succeeded by saying:

"Great job! You sat on the potty!"

You can give negative feedback to let her know she blew it, "No! Come back here. I told you to sit down!" The latter can confuse and overwhelm a child who in fact followed your directions and sat on the potty, if only very briefly.

Giving positive feedback has been likened to handing out warm fuzzies, because acknowledging a child's accomplishments is a wonderful gift. Giving negative feedback has been likened to bestowing cold pricklies, because a child is apt to feel criticized. When you focus on your child's errors, mistakes, and omissions, she may become convinced that, try as she might, she can't get things right. She may give up and stop trying. Many children tune out their parents to the point that they may appear to have hearing problems. Other children adopt an I-don't-care attitude to defend against repeated blows to their egos. If your child seems never to listen to you, the problem may be that he has listened too well and taken your negative comments too much to heart!

If your child doesn't even attempt to sit on the potty when instructed, don't despair. You can still set him up to succeed. For instance, place a Teddy bear on the potty and praise it. Ask your child to pat the bear's head. If he does, encourage his willingness to cooperate by saying, "Yes! Teddy likes that!"

Praise and Pressure

Praise is a type of positive feedback that communicates, "I like that you did that." Praise can help children feel good about themselves, build confidence, and motivate them to repeat certain behaviors. However, when toddlers are grappling with independence issues, they sometimes feel compelled to do the exact opposite of what their parents want. They may take strong exception to praise. Instead of gushing, "You used the potty! Mommy's so proud of you," offhand comments such as, "Aren't you proud of yourself?" or "You should be proud" can be more effective.

Motivating Your Little One

The age-old phrase "put yourself in his shoes" can help moms realize what this experience is like for their tot. It's tough! So, how can you motivate your child? Two main psychological tools increase

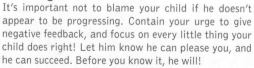

Mommy Knows Best

It's important not to blame your child if he doesn't appear to be progressing. Contain your urge to give negative feedback, and focus on every little thing your child does right! Let him know he can please you, and he can succeed. Before you know it, he will!

motivation. Positive reinforcement involves giving your child something she likes, such as hugs, toys, treats, or praise. Negative reinforcement enables your child to escape or avoid something unpleasant, such as escaping dirty diapers or avoiding an upset mom. As you may have guessed, positive reinforcement is far more effective than negative reinforcement. We can't expect ourselves to be incessantly positive, but we can make an effort to be so most of the time.

Sometimes it's hard to tell when you have provoked your child's flight response. When she says that she doesn't need to use the potty, you may think she is simply lying. You may not realize that fear propelled her to avoid all thoughts about elimination and the potty. Some children get to the point that they tune out their bodies and don't realize they need to relieve themselves, although their parents see the signs very clearly. Some youngsters become so anxious, they are unable to relax their muscles enough to use the potty. They may be unable to urinate for many hours at a stretch, even as they are screaming in pain from an overly full bladder. Others withhold stool, becoming constipated or even encopretic—a condition resulting in chronic, uncontrollable

Mindful Mommy

Keep in mind that threats and punishment during potty training can create fear and mobilize children's fight-or-flight response. Your child may not fight back or flee at the time, but in the future he may avoid the potty or be more aggressive toward others.

soiling. The latter condition is initially very painful. Eventually, the nerve endings of the anus become numb, and children soil without realizing it. It's easy to see why experts' number one potty training rule is never to punish!

Negative Reinforcement

Having clean, dry, and odor-free pants motivates youngsters who dislike wet, messy ones to use the potty. But many toddlers don't mind them. In fact, most youngsters are quite attached to their diapers, wet or dry, smelly or not. In general, young children have no natural aversion to waste. They are likely to smear, mash, pat, and taste it. Although this is normal, it can make them very sick. Don't let them play in waste!

Your Commitment

Hugs, kisses, and other expressions of approval can keep children motivated for potty training. Spending one-on-one time with you will feel like a great reward. When you accompany your youngster to the bathroom and serve as an attentive audience, your presence can provide a powerful incentive for your child to return.

Mindful Mommy

Even negative attention feels better than being ignored, so purposeful wetting and soiling can be ways to get your attention. The solution is to give lots of positive attention if your child so much as goes near the potty. When accidents happen, don't make a fuss.

Poor motivation to use the potty often coincides with poor motivation on the part of parents to keep up with their potty training program. While you may not want to run to the bathroom each time your toddler needs to use it, it is important not to drag your feet in hopes he will decide he can do without company. To stay motivated, remember that you can either drop what you're doing and fulfill your child's request for company, or you can drop what you're doing in a few minutes and spend time cleaning up an accident. Although potty training can interrupt other daily activities, your toddler can't succeed without your consistent attention!

Some experts point out that playing into toddler greed by giving prizes instead of attention warps children's values. So once again, try to find a balance. A printed smiley face is no substitute for your smiling face. If you give treats and toys, it's important to give positive attention, too.

Effective Rewards

Anyone who has ever tried to diet knows how difficult it is to practice self-denial today to reap a reward in a month or two. Therefore, a good reward

Mommy Knows Best

Sometimes stickers, small toys, treats, or special privileges can reduce demands on parents' time. Providing tangible evidence of the child's accomplishment can help instill pride in a job well done. By giving rewards, you remain involved without having to spend so much time sitting in the bathroom with your child.

is something your child can enjoy immediately. Promises of a chance to put a quarter in a grocery store gumball machine tomorrow, to hear an extra bedtime story later in the evening, or to receive a special toy in a week do not motivate most children. It's more effective to offer an on-the-spot hug, sticker, or story.

Modeling

Children relish doing what friends and other family members do. If toddlers regularly see parents using the toilet, they are likely to want to copy them. Saying that using the potty makes them a "big girl" or a "big boy" just like an idolized parent, older sibling, friend, or relative can motivate them!

In fact, modeling is the most potent form of teaching. Having a coach explain how to dribble a ball isn't nearly as effective as having him demonstrate. Children attending day care centers have many opportunities to observe and mimic more accomplished peers, so they often master potty training earlier than stay-at-home children. Similarly, younger siblings learn more quickly if older brothers, sisters, or parents demonstrate. Let your child watch you use

Mommy Must

A fun way to reward potty progress is with a special phone call to Grandma Lois, Uncle Mark, Cousin David, or any family friend willing to "ooh" and "ah" over the latest potty training victory. Put your child on the line, or be sure she listens in as you share the good news. This means a lot to little folks.

the bathroom or find someone else who is willing to serve as a model.

Unfortunately, the prospect of becoming a "big boy" or "big girl" like an older sibling or friend doesn't always strike toddlers as appealing.

While little folks sometimes enjoy the greater freedom, independence, autonomy, and respect that come with using the potty, at other times they grasp the downside—staying clean and dry is a big responsibility. Parents do less for them and expect them to do more for themselves. In fact, the pressures for increased maturity that using the potty demand can cause children to stop progressing or regress in other areas. You can help your child feel better about growing up by reducing other demands, tolerating more clinging, and providing extra doses of TLC.

Controlling Your Emotions

If you feel worried about your child's progress, you're not alone! For many parents, potty training triggers:

- A host of fears ("Will my child ever learn?")
- Feelings of inadequacy ("I must be doing something wrong")
- Insecurity ("Other children her age are trained")
- Frustration ("My child isn't even trying")
- Stress ("I'm tired of these messes!")

These negative emotions can readily combine into a cauldron of smoldering anger. Taking your anger out on your child will make you both feel worse. For everyone's sake, get your feelings out in a different way. Keep reading to learn about ways to calm yourself.

Anger Management Techniques

Use these anger management techniques to calm yourself. Your child may benefit from learning some of them, too.

- Take some slow, deep breaths and count to ten.
- Force yourself to smile. The very act of curving your lips into a grin reduces tension.
- Compile a book of jokes and cartoons that strike you as particularly humorous, and read them when you are upset.
- Find something funny in the situation.
- Drink a cup of chamomile tea.
- Have a turkey sandwich made with whole wheat bread. The tryptophan and carbohydrate combination induces a sense of well-being.
- Put on some lotion scented with real (not artificial) lavender.
- Play some relaxing music, sit down, close your eyes, take some slow, deep breaths, and visualize a relaxing scene, such as a beach, forest, or expanse of blue sky.

- Put your toddler in a stroller and go for a brisk walk. Exert yourself long enough for your system to release endorphins.

A Special Relaxation Technique

When other approaches to relaxing fall short, try a few moments of meditation. You can create a guided meditation for yourself by making an audiotape. Speak the words below into a tape recorder. Pause for a few seconds between each sentence, and insert thirty seconds of silence after each paragraph.

Close your eyes and notice everything that is touching your skin. Notice the feel of the chair on the back of your legs, the sensations of your feet touching the floor, what your hands are touching. Notice the sensations of your clothes touching your body and any small movements of air brushing your face. Try to distinguish the feeling of your hair touching your forehead, ears, or neck.

Become aware of any sounds in the room. Notice any loud noises. Now listen for faint sounds...the hum of an appliance, the whoosh of passing cars, the creak of the floor, the rustle of air moving through the room.

Now concentrate on smells. Try to distinguish any odors in the room. See if you can detect the aroma of food...of the carpeting... of the air from an open window. Try to detect the scent of your skin, makeup, shampoo, or perfume.

Notice any tastes in your mouth. Explore the insides of your cheeks with your tongue. Run your tongue over your teeth and notice the taste.

Open your eyes and look directly ahead. Let your eyes lose focus and relax your eyelids. Without bringing objects into focus or thinking about what you see, notice the colors and shapes before you.

With your eyes still open but unfocused, bring all of the physical sensations you have detected into awareness at once…the sensations on your skin…the sounds in the room…any smells and tastes…the colors and shapes before you.

Close your eyes and slowly count to ten. When you open your eyes, you will feel relaxed and refreshed.

When you feel stressed, sit in a comfortable chair and play your tape. If you can't manage five minutes alone, see if your toddler will sit down and listen with you.

Minds of Their Own

Although adults are responsible for teaching, coaching, and cheerleading, learning to use the potty really is your child's job. Even great teachers cannot make students learn. Even the most skilled coaches cannot force players to win. Even the most enthusiastic cheerleaders cannot motivate a team that isn't intent on victory. There is truth to the old saying, "You can lead a horse to water, but you can't make it drink." Adults may be able to force tots to sit on the potty, but they can't make them use it!

Youngsters have minds, hearts, and wills of their own. They encounter different struggles along the way. Everyone learns in time. Exactly when that happens, however, is up to each child.

Chapter 2

Is My Little One Ready?

TRY TO ADOPT A gradual approach to teaching your little one about elimination and the potty. By talking about both from a very early age, your child will become used to the discussions and will be ready to learn to use the potty when you decide to move forward. Your child's emotional resources and maturity are important factors to consider when you plan a date for completing potty training.

A Lesson in Anatomy

It's time to bone up on everything you never wanted to know about the bowel and bladder so you can understand what is involved in potty training. You will be a better coach and better mommy because of it, so read carefully!

Two muscles shaped like donuts, called sphincters, control the flow of waste from the body. The bladder sphincter controls urine, and the anal sphincter controls bowel movements. When your child contracts a sphincter muscle, the donut closes, keeping urine and/or waste inside the body. When he relaxes a sphincter, the donut opens and waste flows out. Seems simple enough, right? The catch is that to push out waste, children must tense some muscles to start the flow while relaxing the sphincters so it can be released. Children eventually learn how, but this comes with time.

Toddler boys mature more slowly and finish potty training a few months later than girls, on average. Without any training or help, most children achieve nighttime bowel control first. This happens on its own, as a result of physical maturity. Daytime bowel control usually comes next, perhaps because most youngsters have at least one bowel movement at a predictable time each day. The contractions of the intestine signaling the start of a bowel movement are often obvious. Children grunt and pass gas, so it is easy for parents and children alike to recognize when it is time for a potty trip.

During bowel movements both sphincters relax, so children usually urinate and defecate at the same time. By focusing on bowel training, parents can help children become bladder trained at the same time.

Mindful Mommy

You can think of sphincters like dams. When there is too much water, they collapse and there is a flood. Similarly, when the bowel or bladder are overly full, the pressure on the sphincter becomes too great. The muscle collapses, and an accident ensues.

Take a Relaxed Approach, for Everyone's Sake

Like many adults, toddlers do not respond well to pressure. If you are in a hurry or are particularly hard on your little one, your efforts can backfire. Potty training can end up taking much longer than if you adopt a more relaxed approach. If you are potty training a young baby, you must never use any type of pressure. If you have a potty training deadline for your toddler, be sure she:

- Is mature enough to follow directions readily
- Can remain seated for at least five minutes at a stretch
- Enjoys tasks that make her more independent
- Persists when learning is hard
- Can handle frustration
- Can handle occassional accidents without a loss of motivation

Make sure your child isn't in the midst of dealing with other major issues, such as the arrival of a new baby, the loss of a favorite day care teacher, or a move to a new house. One challenge at a time is enough for little people! The rule of thumb is to allow at least a month for a youngster to adapt and settle in after a major life change. Since even minor events such as teething, moving from a crib to a regular bed, or having out-of-town guests can throw tots off balance for a few days or weeks, wait until household routines are re-established and your youngster feels and acts up to par before moving forward with potty training.

Toddlers are very sensitive to parental anxiety and tension, and react negatively to pressure. You may have to accept that potty training is something you can't rush. When you scale back your expectations, you may well speed learning.

Using the Right Vocabulary

Get your child on the right track from the get-go! Children can begin acquiring the potty training vocabulary they need virtually from birth. When you change diapers, talk to your infant about what you are doing so he starts to become familiar with the vocabulary. Decide what words you plan to use, and be consistent. Even older toddlers become confused when parents use different words for the same thing.

You may think it's cute when your toddler uses off-color words and expressions, but other parents and caregivers won't be amused. They may fear your youngster will be a bad influence and not want him around their children. Don't forget to teach the correct

Mindful Mommy

When children first learn to walk, they are excited by their newfound independence. They are also more active. At this stage, children have a hard time following directions and sitting still. To make everyone's life easier, choose a different time to begin potty training.

vocabulary when your child reaches school age. A third grader may not let you know he has a problem because he doesn't know the correct term and is too embarrassed to tell you that his "wee-wee" hurts.

Define Your Terms

Correct Term	Popular Word
Toilet	Potty, Pot
Urine	Pee, Pee-pee, Tinkle, Wee-wee
Urinate	Go pee-pee
Stool, Feces	Poop, Poo-poo, Do-do, Poopy
Defecate, have a bowel movement	Go poo-poo
Penis	Pee-pee, Thing, Privates
Vagina	Bottom, Privates
Buttocks	Bum, Tush, Bottom

Choosing Words

Virtually every toddler goes through the sassy phase of calling people "poopy head" and using other unpleasant putdowns. If you respond with shock, anger, or glee, the attention may encourage him to repeat them. The idea that particular words and expressions can draw such a dramatic response from you will intrigue him.

Jan Faull, in her book *Mommy! I Have to Go Potty!*, suggests telling tykes that potty talk belongs in the bathroom. Take your child there, listen patiently as he repeats the forbidden words and phrases, but don't otherwise encourage him. Conclude your little "bull" session by saying you are available to listen whenever he wants to talk, but these words are for use in the bathroom only. After a few sessions, the novelty of saying the words other kids find so funny is supposed to wear off. Hopefully, he'll stop using them around the house. In actuality, it seems unlikely that toddlers will grasp that it's okay to use certain words in the bathroom but not other places; even preschoolers find coping with two sets of rules very hard. Still, if your child persists in using bathroom words around the house, it may be worth a try.

It may be hard for toddlers to understand that calling people names hurts their feelings. However, even a very young child can learn that it hurts your feelings when he calls you names. Teach your youngster acceptable words to use if he is angry about something, such as, "I'm mad at you, Mom."

Teaching Special Concepts

There are some special concepts your tot needs to know for potty training, especially the difference between wet and dry, and between soiled/messy/dirty and clean. Use these words often while washing and drying your child's hands, cleaning up spills, and wiping spots off of clothing, as well as when changing diapers. As you say, "wet," have your child touch a wet item so she can feel it. Get in the habit of

Mommy Must

If your child keeps saying naughty words, telling him not to talk "that way" is too general. If ignoring his colorful vocabulary doesn't solve the problem, tell him exactly which words you don't like and which ones are okay.

asking if her diaper is wet or dry. Show her how to reach inside her disposable diaper and feel the crotch. After she answers, check her diaper yourself and tell her if she was correct. If she wasn't, give her the correct answer and have her recheck her diaper.

Children also need to know what it means to practice, to relax, to have an accident, and to hurry so they understand what you mean when you say:

"Practice sitting on the potty."
"Practice relaxing on the potty."
"Practice using the potty."
"You had an accident."
"Hurry, so you don't have an accident!"

Practice Makes Perfect!

Use the words, "practice," "hurry," and "relax" in your child's everyday life whenever possible to help your child learn this essential potty training vocabulary. To teach that practice is the route to improving, use the word "practice" whenever your child is doing something again and again to achieve a goal. For example:

"You're practicing eating with a spoon. You're learning to use it."
"You're practicing climbing the stairs. You're getting better at climbing."
"You're practicing putting the puzzle together. You've almost got it!"

If your child understands, "Practice sitting on the potty," she'll be less likely to feel punished when told it's time to practice. Once she understands that the goal is to practice sitting and relaxing, hopefully, she won't become frustrated if she doesn't succeed in using the potty instantly.

When children sit on the potty, many don't use it because they are too tense. When the potty session ends and they are allowed to get up, they relax. Their sphincter muscles relax, too, and they have an accident. Having your child sit on the potty is not enough. He must be relaxed in order to be able to use it. To teach the concept of "relaxing," simply point out examples of when people (including you and your tot) are relaxed. When your youngster is calm and comfortable so he can learn to associate his feelings and sensations with the word, say:

"You look relaxed"

Teaching him how to relax is harder. When he is upset, suggest he take some deep breaths, sit quietly, and think about something that makes him feel calm. Your tot will soon get the idea!

Hurry Up!

Most parents use the expression "hurry up" so often, children know all too well what it means. Getting them to hurry to the potty can be tricky. Constantly pressuring your child to move quickly may cause him to ignore you or worse: to resist and throw on the brakes. Telling her to "Hurry to the potty" may cause her to move more slowly or run the other way. Try to let your child move at her own pace, and only urge her to hurry when something truly important demands it. Slowing down is hard for busy families, but it is good for everybody!

Once children have mastered these concepts, they're well on the way to being potty trained even if they haven't tried sitting on the potty yet. Don't underestimate the importance of teaching the basics!

Giving Directions

When your child knows a basic phrase, such as, "Go to . . ." she will more readily understand a specific direction, such as, "Go to the potty." If she is very young, doesn't hear well, or has some other communication difficulty, she must understand your gestures and signals so you can communicate with her. Give basic directions often to prepare your child for potty training, and be patient. Most parents think their children understand much more than they actually do!

Directions They'll Understand	
Teach your child...	So your child will understand...
"Go to...."	"Go to the potty."
"Tell me when you need/want..."	"Tell me when you need the potty."
"Get some..."	"Get some toilet paper/clean pants/ a sponge/the potty bowl."
"Wipe..."	"Wipe yourself" and "Wipe up the floor."

Toddlers are still learning to make sense of one-step directions, such as, "Go to the potty."

Two-step directions, such as, "Go to the bathroom and sit down on the potty" may be too much for them.

During potty training, wait until your child completes one step before telling him to do something else. If your child is not emotionally and psychologically ready, nothing will be accomplished—don't forget the story of Jenna and her second child!

Getting Along

If your little one understands verbal directions, you're off to a great start. But understanding directions is one thing; following them is quite another. Many young toddlers are too busy exploring to sit on the potty. As older toddlers become increasingly intent on pursuing their own interests, they may become less reliable about doing what they're told.

Teach your child to do what you say so that she will eventually follow potty training instructions. Let your child know which behaviors you like and which ones you do not. Comment on small successes, and avoid focusing on the times when she isn't doing what she's been told. If you say, "Don't spill your milk!" and she glances at her cup, say, "Good! You're being careful." Later, if the milk gets spilled, give her a sponge so she can help clean it up—and acknowledge her. Similarly, if she's tormenting the cat, show her how to pet it gently. Then praise her for being nice to the kitty.

Of all the directions toddlers need to follow during potty training, one of the hardest is to relax while sitting on the potty. Sitting still is hard at this very active age. Fortunately, even hyperactive children stay seated for short stretches, such as in a high chair, car seat, or grocery cart, as well as while watching videos, listening to stories, or playing with toys. When your child is sitting still, point it out so he knows he can do it!

Although it may be hard, try to ignore your child's restless hands and feet, and his squirms and wiggles. Reprimanding your youngster will increase his nervousness, which will cause him to fidget more, not less. Instead, be positive! Help your child recognize that sitting is something he can do by praising him regularly for staying seated. Point out successes whether they occur in the playroom or the grocery store, and hold small celebrations:

"You sat in the grocery cart for five minutes! Congratulations! You're learning! How about a ride on the mechanical pony to celebrate?"

Mommy Knows Best

If your child is especially contrary and rebellious, learn the fine art of setting and enforcing limits before you attempt potty training. You can read "The Everything® Toddler Book" or another book on discipline, or take a parenting course.

Chances are that he'll soon be working to impress you with his ability to sit—assuming he can release energy through physically active play before and after. Be sure he gets plenty of exercise!

Too many parents assume that their child is having trouble remaining seated on the potty due to hyperactivity. Children are full of energy, and most don't get enough exercise. Turn off the television, eliminate caffeine, and make sure your child has lots of time for active play before you ask him to sit on the potty.

Helping Tots Recognize When It's Potty Time

At three months of age, babies can distinguish the sensation of needing to pass waste. They actually cry or give another signal before they wet or soil to alert their parents. In the days before diapers, parents responded quickly so their babies didn't wet or soil themselves. Yet many toddlers have great difficulty sorting out their bodily sensations. Disposable diapers mask wetness and obscure the cause-and-effect relationship between elimination and dampness. Over time, children lose touch with their bodies. Start potty training your next child when she's a baby or an infant!

Teach your toddler to recognize the sensations that occur during elimination by noticing when she is relieving herself and commenting. If she is always clad in a diaper, noticing can be difficult. Some children make a face or assume a special posture. Some older toddlers stand with their feet slightly apart and look down. If your child regularly urinates shortly after awakening from a nap or after eating, remove the diaper and see if she will sit on the potty for a bit. If she urinates while sitting on the potty, point out what is happening, and praise her. If you can't tell when your child is urinating, remove her diaper, let the accident happen, and use it as a teaching opportunity. Many children have never seen themselves urinating. It is usually easier to tell when a child is having a bowel movement. Talk her through the whole process to help to increase her awareness of what is happening.

Even if you feel uncomfortable talking about elimination, it is important to describe exactly what is happening so your child can learn·

"Do you smell that? You're passing gas. You're going to have a B.M."

"You're grunting. The B.M. is coming. Someday you'll go to the potty when you start grunting."

"You're putting your B.M. in your diaper."

Mindful Mommy

Don't only ask your little one whether her urine or B.M. is coming out when the answer is yes! She may say, "No" to avoid diaper changes and end up confused. Ask at other times, too. Congratulate her for giving the right answer. Correct her gently if she's wrong.

"You're all through having a B.M."

"Your diaper smells. We need to put on a clean one."

"See? Your B.M. is in your diaper. I'm going to throw it away. Bye-bye, B.M.!"

"I'm wiping your bottom to clean it. When you're bigger, you'll clean your bottom with toilet paper."

"See? This diaper is clean. You smell nice now that your diaper is clean."

Problem-Solving Techniques

Everyone is bound to make mistakes now and then! Young children are virtually guaranteed to have some accidents during potty training. Unfortunately, some youngsters overreact. Those with poor self-esteem, difficulties tolerating frustration, and little perfectionists may feel defeated and give up trying to learn. Help your child develop better persistence by offering a little help and a lot of encouragement whenever he is struggling with any task, such as trying to fit a block into a hole, to retrieve a toy that is just out of reach, to get his pants on, etc. Provide as little hands-on help as necessary.

- Encourage him by saying: "Almost...you've almost got it . . . hang in there..."
- And if he succeeds, reward him in a happy tone, "You kept trying and you succeeded!"

- If he didn't quite make it, provide comfort and reassurance. Tell him, "Keep practicing! Tomorrow it should be easier."

Little perfectionists may persist well enough, but their lack of patience with themselves and worries about making mistakes can translate into more rather than fewer accidents. Tension and anxiety increase the urinary urge and can prevent children from emptying the bladder completely, so they need to urinate more frequently. Begin teaching the complicated process of handling mistakes in all your child's learning situations, not just those that involve potty training. The steps include seeking help, noting when something went wrong, fixing whatever needs mending, and deciding what to do differently next time to avoid the same mistake. A better attitude toward mistakes will translate to a better attitude toward potty training accidents. It can strengthen motivation to keep trying when the going gets tough.

Children are born mimics, so a good way to teach the problem-solving steps is to verbalize your thoughts when you make a mistake. Try saying some of the following things.

Mommy Must

When your child has an accident, help him focus on the lesson, not the mistake. Once he grasps that accidents aren't the end of the world, it will be easier for him to recover and move on.

"Oops, I dropped the tea cup! Now I have to clean up the broken pieces. It slipped because my hands are wet. Next time I'll dry them before I pick up a cup."

"Oops, I pinched your finger in the seatbelt! Can I kiss it to make it better? Next time I'll be sure your hands are out of the way before I buckle you in."

Similarly, when your child has an accident, whether during potty training or at another time, help her understand what went wrong, explain how to repair any damage (having her participate if possible), and suggest how to avoid the problem in the future. For example, you might say:

"Uh-oh, your dress is wet. We need to wipe up the floor and change your clothes. You didn't pull up your skirt before you sat on the potty. I need to show you how and help you practice so your dress won't get wet next time."

Boosting Motivation

We all enjoy a little praise sometimes. It makes us more confident and willing to try new things. For children to be motivated to master the potty, it helps if they take pride in achievements that make them more independent. Commend your tot for participating in her own care while you are feeding, dressing, and bathing her.

"You put your shirt on by yourself! Such a big girl!"

"You're learning to use a spoon just like Daddy."

Most toddlers go back and forth about wanting to grow up. The truth is that they are still babies. They need to know they can still count on you for comfort and support. Allow your tot to crumble into your arms when he feels overwhelmed instead of insisting that he act like a big boy. Provide gentle nudges toward independence, but don't push!

Cleanliness

While many adults can't stand being in muddy jeans, children may not mind soiled clothes. In fact, children lack an inborn aversion to human waste, so the chance to avoid messy, smelly diapers doesn't provide much of an incentive to use the potty. Children who wear disposable diapers usually don't feel the wetness, so they aren't motivated to keep them dry. However, if your youngster often removes his diaper or alerts you when he needs to be changed, he is a good candidate for potty training.

Cloth diapers can enhance youngsters' motivation for potty training if they dislike being wet. It's a good idea to switch from disposable to cloth diapers before potty training. However, some children don't mind cold, wet diapers. Every tot is different!

Using the potty is more sanitary than wearing diapers. The bacteria in human waste produce ammonia, which harms the skin and can cause serious rashes. Encourage an appreciation for cleanliness by expressing pleasure over how nice your child looks and smells after a bath or diaper change.

Experts advise against expressing disgust over dirty diapers and human waste. If a child feels ashamed, he may not want to admit to you when he needs to use the potty. You definitely need your child to tell you when he needs help to go to the bathroom!

Put Things Where They Belong

Is your child interested in putting toys and small objects into boxes and cans? Does she enjoy fitting blocks into the correct slots on three-dimensional puzzles? Some experts believe that toddlers who like to put one thing inside another, arrange objects, line up toys, and keep things in order may be more motivated for potty training.

Certainly if your child fusses when a household object isn't in the "right" place, you can capitalize on his desire for order. Mention when you need to use the toilet and explain that you are going to put your urine or B.M. "in the potty where it belongs." When

Mindful Mommy

Some children don't like diapers because the bulk between their legs inhibits movement. If your youngster persists in removing his diaper, it's probably time to move forward with potty training.

changing soiled diapers, mention that, "Children are supposed to put their B.M.s in the potty," and add that when he gets bigger he'll be able to put his B.M.s in the potty, too. Have your child watch as you scrape a soiled diaper into the toilet and explain, "This is where a B.M. belongs." If he is diaperless and begins to relieve himself, see if he can stop while you take him to the potty, so he can put it in the "right" place. Not all children can stop urinating once they have started, but some can. Even if your child cannot stop, you can begin implanting the idea that urine is supposed to go in the potty.

Physical Readiness

You may be waiting, counting the days even, until your toddler is potty trained. There are several physical skills your child needs to achieve potty independence. Toddlers need to be able to get their pants up and down quickly. This skill is difficult, and accidents while struggling to remove clothes are common. Have your toddler participate in dressing and undressing as much as possible. Guide her hands to teach the correct motions for raising and lowering pants.

Mindful Mommy

Undoing snaps, unzipping zippers, opening Velcro tabs, and maneuvering small buttons out of buttonholes are big challenges for little fingers. Give lots of encouragement when your child practices, and don't hurry her.

Asking for Help

Youngsters require a lot of help during the initial phases of potty training, so they must be willing to reach out to others. Teach your child to solicit your assistance. Ask her to call when she needs your help with something, and attentively respond to her requests.

Both the ability and the desire to imitate others will speed potty training. Many children learn by watching peers, parents, or a doll go through the process. Because younger siblings like to follow older ones around the house and are motivated to do what they do, younger children are usually trained at earlier ages. Some manage to learn with very little formal instruction.

Bladder Control

Although every child is different, many youngsters achieve daytime continence by age one, according to a 1993 report in the journal *Current Problems in Pediatrics*. In fact, most children of the world finish potty training soon after they learn to walk. Parents recognize

Mommy Knows Best

Children are copycats. They learn many lessons by watching others and trying to do what they do. Wanting to be like Mommy and Daddy can serve as an important potty training incentive. Let your youngster observe you using the bathroom.

when their infant is about to eliminate and respond by holding a little pot under the baby to catch the waste. They also make a special sound as the baby eliminates. Once the baby learns the sound, parents can avoid accidents by cueing their infant to eliminate.

Older Babies

As your toddler grows, so does her bladder. As a result, she will urinate less often than when she was a baby. Once she figures out how to calm bladder contractions and tighten the bladder sphincter to hold in urine, she can stave off urination for longer periods. It will take her a while to discover how long she can actually "hold it" once she feels the urge to urinate. Since "holding it" for too long leads to accidents and can even damage the bladder, it's important that she not delay when she needs to go potty.

Toddlers can make themselves urinate once they figure out how to push by tensing one set of muscles while relaxing the sphincter muscle so the urine can come out. Until then, telling them to "try" to use the potty may not help, because they tend to tense all of their muscles, including the sphincter. All you can do is try to have your child seated on the potty at the right time and point out when your child is urinating in an effort to increase his awareness.

You can estimate bladder functioning by watching for these signs:

Your child's diapers remain dry for one to two hours at a stretch during the day. More frequent urination makes training more difficult. Note that if your child leaks urine, this may be due to a physical problem. Often, the cause is a bladder infection. See your doctor immediately.

Your child urinates large quantities at one time. This signals that the sphincter is able to contain urine properly. If the stream is not strong and steady when your child urinates heavily, notify your doctor.

Your child can stop the flow of urine midstream. Not all toddlers can, but having mastered this tricky maneuver means they can tense and relax the bladder sphincter at will. This can reduce the number of accidents—assuming they can remember how to stop when the urge to urinate is strong.

Your child awakens in response to a full bladder. This awakening means the sensations of bladder fullness are strong enough to rouse the sleeping brain. Children who cannot wake up when the bladder is full have problems with bedwetting.

Your child awakens dry after naps and/or in the morning. This suggests that bladder size is normal and that urine production decreased during sleep, as it should. If hormone levels are insufficient to suppress urine production, children must make many trips to the bathroom during the night to keep from wetting the bed.

It is obvious when your child is about to urinate or defecate. It's not always obvious, but if it is, it will be easier to help your youngster get to the potty in time.

Although children can develop good bladder control during the first year or two of life if they are worked with consistently, an occasional daytime accident is to be expected until age three. Bedwetting can remain a problem if the sensation of a full bladder isn't strong enough to awaken them. Even at age five, approximately 15 to 20 percent of youngsters continue to wet the bed.

Learning to Control B.M.s

Bowel contractions reflexively expel solid waste (the meconium) during the first day or two of life. Soon after, many infants can be observed pushing to help a bowel movement along. They have three to nine movements per day, depending on how often they eat. Breast milk usually causes looser stool than formula. As children mature, they have fewer bowel movements each day.

Bowel training is much easier if the stool is well formed. Children won't have enough warning to get to the bathroom on time if they have very loose stool or diarrhea. It is important that children not be constipated during potty training because hard stool can be painful. Many youngsters associate the pain with

Mommy Knows Best

Some toddlers have several bowel movements each day; some average less than one a day. Each child is different. The consistency of the stool is more important than the frequency. Stool that is too hard or too loose complicates potty training.

the potty and become fearful of it. Extreme constipation can cause uncontrollable leakage as watery stool seeps around the hard mass and out the rectum. See your doctor if your child has this condition. Bowel training is also much easier if your child can tell when a bowel movement is starting. Most toddlers can push willfully to help bowel movements along but may not know how simultaneously to relax the sphincter muscle to release stool. As with controlling the bladder, learning how to tense some muscles while relaxing others can be hard for children to master.

Parent Readiness

While you have to commit to working on potty training for as long as it takes, you might be happily surprised. Some children need only a couple of lessons! To make it easier on yourself though, make sure you have a plan.

Potty training will be easier and faster if you decide in advance what your child needs to learn and how you will teach it. No matter what method you use, the keys are kindness and consistency. To help ensure you remain kind, choose a time when you feel emotionally centered and can be patient. Otherwise, your child is likely to react to your tension and have difficulty concentrating. Wanting something and being ready for it are two different things. Many parents who want their child to be trained by a particular age or before a special deadline soon discover they don't have the time or energy required to achieve their goal.

Daring to Differ

Perhaps Mom wants "her" child to experience a later, softer, gentler approach to potty training while Dad thinks that kind of coddling will ruin him for life. Or, Mom may be sick of laundry and want to get this potty training show on the road, but Dad is saying she'll break his spirit by pushing too hard. How can a couple reconcile two such different philosophies?

Battling for control of your child's bowel and bladder accomplishes nothing. If you and your spouse don't see eye to eye, the potty practice method (which you will read about later in this book) may be a program you can agree upon. For this method, your child is required to sit on the potty for about five minutes when he's likely to need to use it (on awakening, after meals, and every hour or two at other times). He can avoid having to sit on the potty if he uses it on his own beforehand. He can end his potty practice session sooner if he uses the potty and washes his hands. If that method isn't agreeable to both of

Mindful Mommy

Potty training can be stressful for everyone in your family. Try not to argue with your spouse over which method is better. Whether you choose a laid back or aggressive approach, rehashing the pros and cons won't speed potty training!

you, consider letting the indulgent parent handle the laundry and use the potties-without-pressure method for six months, then have the stricter parent give the potty practice or fast-track method a whirl. Agree to support one another no matter which of you is in charge. It is important to respect what each of you has to offer.

In-home Helper

Many people feel uncomfortable discussing intimate bodily functions. It can make parents feel as if they're breaking a taboo. Their desire not to discuss this delicate subject can create real problems if your child has worries, anxieties, or concerns about having bowel movements in the potty. Many children do.

One way to make discussions easier is to begin by reading the storybook *Everybody Poops* to your child. The book's straightforward explanations can be shocking to adults "An elephant makes a big poop/ A mouse makes a tiny poop."

You may find the cartoon pictures of animal poop and the contents of a soiled diaper too graphic for your taste. Yet, most children find the book engaging. Sharing this book with your child can prepare you for the kind of frank discussions about potties and elimination you will need to have. Because it answers their unspoken questions and relieves their anxieties, it has served as a miracle cure for many nervous toddlers. It can be particularly effective in helping them overcome feelings of shame about using the potty. Shame is a major force behind some children's staunch refusal to have bowel movements in the potty. These youngsters may hide in corners, behind sofas, or seek out other private places.

Kindness and Consistency

As stated before, the two basic rules of potty training are kindness and consistency. To provide consistency, have all caregivers participate, use the same approach, and work on potty training regularly. When training is sporadic, children become confused as to what is expected of them. The habit of using the potty takes much longer to develop.

Consistency can be especially hard to come by if your child spends a lot of time with other caregivers. This situation is undoubtedly part of the reason that so many children are now trained so late. An adult must be responsible for prompting them until using the potty becomes a habit. Otherwise, youngsters have to remain conscious of their bladder at every moment. That takes more energy and concentration than most little folks can muster.

Make sure to brief other caregivers on what method you are using with your little one, and ask that they stick to it when they are in charge. There are several things you can do to increase the likelihood that other adults will follow your program:

1. Write out exactly what you're doing at home or buy more copies of this book, bookmark the chapters, and underline the relevant passages

that day care center teachers, baby sitters, and the "other parent" need to know.

2. Set aside some uninterrupted time with other caregivers to discuss potty training so you're both on the same page.

3. Make it easy for others to cooperate by supplying everything they need to be able to follow your rules. For instance, for the potty practice method, provide a list of times to take your child to the potty.

4. Provide a kitchen timer that caregivers can set to remind themselves when it's time for another potty trip, and to signal your child when he can get off the potty a few minutes later. Provide a calendar for keeping track of successes and accidents, a stock of rewards, a sticker chart, and extra changes of clothes in case of accidents.

Hygiene Training

Potty training is not just about learning to eliminate into a special receptacle. It is about maintaining a clean environment in order to prevent illness

Mommy Knows Best

Most children respond well to consistency and dislike change. Many children will use their potty at home but refuse to use strange ones. Try a portable potty. If your child becomes accustomed to using it at home, he may be willing to use it other places, too.

and safeguard health, as well as maintaining good personal hygiene so as not to offend others. Parents and other caregivers need to teach youngsters the procedures to follow for wiping, flushing, potty-bowl rinsing, and hand washing. Good personal hygiene comes from consistent training.

Most tots are eager to comply. For them, tearing off and using toilet paper is lots of fun.

Let your child help doing the following things:

- Carrying the potty bowl to the toilet and emptying it
- Flushing the toilet
- Closing the lid
- Turning on the water faucet
- Using soap to wash up
- Turning off the water faucet
- Drying hands

Curb your urge to rush your child through the cleanup process, and avoid accusing her of "just playing." These moments are often the best rewards, and they can make the chore of learning to use the potty worthwhile. Letting her clean up at her leisure can be a good way to make sure she maintains an upbeat, positive attitude. And with all that scrubbing, she is doing important work!

Chapter 3

What Do We Need to Get Started?

SPECIAL POTTY TRAINING STORYBOOKS, videos, dolls, underpants, potty chairs, and stepping stools thrill toddlers. These great new toys can help motivate them to leave diapers behind and join the world of big people. Whenever possible, let your child help choose the potty training products she likes.

Different Types of Potties

You and your child may love the dolls that wet, or you may want to read all of the potty books you can find. That's fine, but the only thing you really need to teach your tot is a little pot! Although a number of commercial products can make life easier, a potty is the only must-have item for potty training. In days gone by, a simple bowl sufficed. The added comfort and appealing colors of commercial products undeniably enhance toddlers' motivation. Shopping at garage sales and discount stores can be a good way to save money.

Two basic types of commercial potties are available for sale. Potty chairs are self-contained units that sit on the floor. They are low enough to increase children's feelings of security. Having a potty chair to call her own, for her exclusive use, may increase your toddler's interest. The disadvantage is that potty chairs have a removable bowl. The bowl must be carried to the toilet, emptied, and rinsed after each use. Also, some children struggle with the transition from the potty chair to the regular toilet. Potty seats attach to the seat of a regular toilet, creating a smaller opening so children don't fall in. Some toddlers like the feeling of being grown up that comes from using the toilet like older siblings and parents, but some youngsters are afraid of the height. Climbing up can be difficult, and a scary fall can complicate training. The biggest drawback is the lack of support for the feet, which children need to get enough leverage to push for bowel movements.

Take your youngster with you when you buy a potty so you can check the fit and hopefully choose one he likes. Here are some features to look for:

Mindful Mommy

A simple pot will work for potty training. Find one that is short enough so that your child's feet rest comfortably on the ground, narrow enough at the top so he doesn't fall in, and with a wide base so it doesn't tip over. The top rim should be wide so as not to cut off circulation in the legs.

Stability—The base of a potty chair should be at least as wide as the top for toddlers, and wider at the base than the top for babies. Have your youngster lean in all directions while sitting on it to make sure that the chair doesn't wobble.

Splashguards—Although splashguards are a boon for sanitation by directing the stream of urine, which is especially useful for boys, many tots end up with a painful bump at some point, and won't want to go near the potty afterward. Climbing over a splashguard to get off the potty seat can be tricky enough to cause a fall. Splashguards should be padded or detachable. Otherwise, make sure there is an inch between the splashguard and the child's crotch.

Security—Potty seats should fasten to the toilet seat securely. Check the grips.

Potty bowl—Bigger is better for preventing spills. The bowl should be easy enough to remove so that toddlers can learn to empty it on their own.

Seat—A cold, hard seat is less inviting than a soft one. Look for a model with a cushioned seat.

Arm rests—If potty chairs have arm rests, children will automatically reach for one and lean on it as they sit down, which can cause the chair to over-turn. Avoid them unless the chair is sufficiently stable.

Stepping stool—Some potty chairs convert to step-ping stools, so children can use them to climb onto the toilet when they are ready to tackle it. Some potty seats have attached stepping stools for ease in climbing up onto the toilet. They serve as a footrest and provide leverage during bowel movements.

Transition options—Some potty chairs convert to potty seats, which can save money down the road.

Musical potties—Some potties play a song when wet, so parents know when their child has urinated. However, babies twist around to see where the music is coming from, which creates a mess and increases the chance of a fall. Musical potties can work well for toddlers, however.

Portability—Some potty chairs and seats fold down for traveling. Be sure that the hinges are sturdy so the unit won't collapse during normal use.

Some children completely reject one potty, refusing even to go near it, yet are very taken with another brand. When shopping, ask about the return policy and save your receipt!

Helped Training Aids

Even though a potty chair or potty seat is all you need, there are some training aids that will make potty training a bit easier, and may even be fun! The training method you use, the age and temperament of your child, your budget, and your own comfort with coaching your child will determine what items you buy. Although the following potty training aids are not essential, they may ease and speed learning:

Baby doll—A doll that wets and comes with its own underpants and baby bottle can be useful for teaching about elimination and demonstrating the process of using the potty.

Baby wipes—When wiping themselves after a bowel movement, children do a better job with moistened towelettes than toilet paper.

Books—Storybooks about potties can increase children's interest, teach the process, and help them to resolve their tangled emotions about giving up diapers.

To help your child's motivation as well as your own, do what you can to make the learning experience fun for both of you.

Clothes for Tots in Training

It's easy to overlook the simple things about potty training when you and your little one are focused on the ultimate goal. So, although it might not seem obvious at first, your child's ability to undress and dress herself will play a role in her progress. A good potty training wardrobe consists of clothes toddlers can remove easily and quickly.

Pull-ups

Most parents automatically buy disposable pull-ups, or disposable training pants as they are sometimes called, but these aren't usually a good idea.

Disposables are so absorbent that youngsters have a hard time feeling the wetness, which slows learning. Disposables also keep them from experiencing the cold, damp discomfort of wet cloth, which can help motivate them to stay dry. While disposables are more likely to thwart potty training than help it along, they can be useful as nightwear for children who resist wearing diapers but continue to wet the bed.

Between Diapers and Underpants

The problem with going straight from diapers to underwear is that there are bound to be some accidents. Cloth training pants, which look like underwear but have additional padding at the crotch, help lessen the mess.

Potty on Discreet Strips (PODS) can be helpful, too. PODS adhere to your child's underpants using an adhesive strip, like that on a sanitary napkin. Although they are absorbent enough to contain the trickles and puddles, they allow children to feel the wetness from an accident. PODS also allow air circulation through the underpants, so the pads quickly cool. That's a much better deterrent to accidents than the warm, cozy feeling of wet disposable diapers.

Mindful Mommy

Just as adults are excited to buy and wear new things, many toddlers are very motivated by the opportunity to wear regular underpants. Let your child choose a kind she likes. Action figures and cartoon characters are popular.

Outfitting Your Tot

Choose clothing that is easy for your tot to get on and off! Pants with elastic waistbands and Velcro closures are easiest for tots. Zippers and snaps are harder; buttons are hardest. Learning to pull tight pants over a round bottom is a challenge, so provide oversized jeans, warm-up pants, slacks, and rompers. Skirts are ideal for girls.

Make sure your child has lots of chances to practice getting his clothes on and off. If you let him help when you dress and undress him, he'll get good practice, and going to the potty will be less challenging. Although you may be in a hurry when you are dressing and undressing him, try not to rush him. He needs to practice to develop the fine motor coordination skills he needs.

How to Reward Your Little One

If smiles and applause as you strive to keep your child motivated for potty training seem to be losing their charm, don't fret! A little treat can sometimes spark motivation. Regardless of which treats or rewards you decide to offer, be sure to stock up in advance!

Mommy Knows Best

When you're dressing your child, remember that long tops get wet during accidents. Although tops can be rolled up and pinned to help keep them dry, short tops are ideal.

- Stickers to affix to a wall chart, calendar, or even to the potty itself. Print out a free chart from *www.DrSonna.org*.
- A coin to drop in the piggy bank or home gum-ball machine.
- A chance to select a wrapped gift from a basket, grab-bag style.
- A small toy. Hot Wheels are a favorite with boys.
- An M&M, raisin, or small candy. Though motivating kids with junk food really is not a good idea, a sweet treat is the only reward that really interests some youngsters.

Children are often ambivalent about the potty because they lose the special, undivided attention they used to get during diaper changes. To make up for the loss of these precious moments and to reward potty successes, read a book, play a game of pat-a-cake, or sing "Itsy-Bitsy Spider" afterward. Make time for your tot so he doesn't feel he's loosing anything and can enjoy his increased independence!

Safety in the Bathroom

The bathroom is one of the rooms that you and your spouse may have skipped when you were baby proofing the house. Once formal potty training begins, youngsters will be spending a lot of time there! It is important to turn the space into a safe place for your baby. Place a teetering toddler high on a potty seat in a cramped space with slippery floors and hard porcelain sink and toilet, and her risk of getting hurt in a fall increases dramatically. Try these baby-proofing methods:

- Outfit floors with skid-proof flooring and mats.
- Place a carpet around the potty to cushion falls.
- Place rubberized decals on the sides of the tub and toilet.
- Clear a path from your child's bedroom to the toilet.
- Put a safety clip on the toilet seat to deter toddlers from playing in the toilet.

Babies and young toddlers must be supervised in the bathroom at all times. Even with careful baby proofing, the bathroom may be too dangerous for wobbly walkers to handle alone, especially if they like to climb. Consider moving the potty chair to another room of the house.

Water Safety

Babies and toddlers can drown by falling into toilet bowls—even children who can swim panic. With their faces in the water, they can't make a sound. Too many parents don't discover what has happened until it's too late. Do not let your child use the toilet unsupervised!

Toddlers find the toilet bowl irresistible. Their splashing makes the floor slippery, which increases the danger of falling down or in. Teach other family members to keep the bathroom door closed at all times. If you use a potty seat, you must remain present to make sure your baby doesn't try to stand on it or decide to play in her waste, which youngsters find fascinating.

If children are getting used to using the potty, they may wake up in the night and want to go. Use night-lights to illuminate the bedroom, hall, and bathroom to eliminate fears of the dark and ease the way for your nighttime traveler. Glow-in-the-dark adhesive strips or a special potty light not only illuminate the path, but also may be novel enough to draw your child toward the target.

What You Really Need

The two most important things you need right now cannot be bought in a store—a ready and willing child and a positive mental attitude. Unfortunately, there's not much that can be done about the former.

Mommy Must

Stay close at hand when your child is sitting on an adult toilet. Besides the risk of drowning, a tumble into cold water can cause a phobia. If you cannot afford a special potty chair or seat, place a small pot or bowl on the floor for your child to use.

Some youngsters delight in new experiences and eagerly embrace change, while others cling to tried-and-true habits and routines, and are very reluctant to let them go. What you can do something about is your attitude.

Since your child will in fact be potty trained, the question really is not whether or not you will achieve your final goal, but how. The following chapters describe very different methods. Whichever you choose, promise yourself that come what may, you will remain committed to enjoying the time you spend with your child. If you keep your promise, you will have the most valuable potty training aid of all.

Chapter 4

Is It Ever Too Early to Start Training? The Baby-Track Method

IT'S BACK TO THE future with the baby-track method. These age-old techniques prove that teaching children to use the potty isn't that different from teaching them to talk or use a spoon. Early exposure and consistent practice help children master important new skills in many areas, including in using the potty.

Early Learning Benefits

To boost your child's language development, you talk, sing songs, and recite nursery rhymes to your baby, even though he doesn't understand you. Similarly, to teach your baby to feed himself, you let him hold the spoon, never mind that he waves it like a flag and makes a mess. Yet when it comes to potty training, most people suggest waiting to begin until age two, claiming that younger children aren't ready to learn. If this same logic were applied to eating, no youngster would be allowed to hold a spoon until around age four, when most have enough control to learn quickly. In truth, the best way to ease and speed learning during the toddler years is to start teaching long before then. You could even end up with a potty trained baby!

The baby-track method simply involves providing a series of relaxed, fun early learning experiences that instill healthy attitudes toward elimination and the potty, teach important concepts, and help your child practice basic potty skills.

Many babies actually begin using the potty or another receptacle regularly after they've been on the baby-track for a short time. There is nothing to suggest that they are hurt by such an early introduction, and much to suggest that they benefit immensely. In fact, during the 1920s, parents in the United States began potty training their infants at three to ten months of age. Parents kept track of their babies' patterns of elimination. When it was about time for them to relieve themselves, parents held them over a sink, basin, toilet, potty, or other receptacle, caught their waste, and rewarded them with coos, kisses, and hugs.

A Compassionate Approach

Potty training fashions come and go, and the favored age for potty training has risen dramatically over the last century. Claudine Brown, mother of two, worked with dozens of children at an orphanage in the 1930s. She reports that the accepted practice was to begin accustoming children to the potty soon after they learned to walk. A few months later, they still needed help with clothing and had an occasional accident. But for all intents and purposes, they were trained. Since one of Brown's nephews learned to walk at a very young age, he was potty trained at eight months!

The period from birth to age three is a critical time for psychological development. The self-concept and feelings of self-worth children acquire during these few short years can continue into adulthood. If caregivers react with even mild frustration, disappointment, or irritation, babies detect their negative emotions. Given the intimate nature of elimination, parents' impatience and anger during potty training can have harmful, far-reaching consequences. When working with a baby, you must be supportive and gentle! Unfortunately, toilet training accidents are the leading catalyst of serious abuse of children over age one, according to a 1994 article in *Your Health* entitled, "The Potty Wars." If you need

Mindful Mommy

Many parents assume the techniques used for training babies must have been harsh and punitive, but this was not the case at all. Mistreating children doesn't help them progress. In fact, it slows them down. Kindness is essential!

help keeping your cool, try the calming techniques in Chapter 1. Brown says, "The keys to working with little ones are time, persistence, patience, and lots of love and understanding."

Sphincter Control

Because it is now fashionable to wait until age two to start potty training, many parents believe younger children are simply not ready. Many Western doctors think that sphincter control does not develop until late in the toddler years. One American author claimed that babies cannot be potty trained because they "leak." The research and success of traditional potty training practices prove that such modern "wisdom" is wrong. Throughout most of the world, parents still catch infants' waste in little pots. Babies sit on the potty for short periods once they can sit up unassisted, and finish training well before age two.

Babies urinate frequently but do not leak. As the bladder grows, it does hold more liquid. Fewer trips to the potty are required when urination is less frequent. However, because babies learn readily, baby training remains the method of choice in most other countries. It is again gaining popularity in the United States.

Baby Basic Skills

You may be wondering how this all works—so let's get to it! Even if babies are too young to have the physical ability or attention span to sit on the potty, parents can do other things to help them learn basic potty vocabulary and concepts.

- When you go the toilet, place your baby on a blanket on the floor near you, and explain what you are doing as you pull down underpants, sit down, urinate or have a B.M., get toilet paper, wipe, flush, and wash up. With many repetitions, babies will understand the vocabulary and process.

- Talk your baby through diaper changes, being careful to keep the vocabulary consistent. "Let's see if your diaper is wet. Is it wet? I'm feeling your diaper. Yes! It's wet." "Let's see if your diaper has B.M. in it. Does it? Yes, I smell the B.M.! Mommy needs to change it. She's taking off your diaper. See the B.M.? (Hold up the diaper.) This is baby's B.M. Yes it is!"

- When teaching the names for parts of the body (e.g., "Where is Baby's tummy?" There it is!"), add the genitals. For example, "Where is Baby's penis? There it is!" "Where is Baby's bottom? There it is!"

- When teaching the function of body parts (e.g., "How does Baby see? With his eyes!" "How does Baby hear? With his ears!"), add, "How does Baby make pee-pee? With his penis!"

- Conclude each diaper change by cleaning your baby's hands with water or a baby wipe so she starts forming the habit of washing after she uses the potty.

If your baby commonly begins wetting or releasing stool when diapers are off, keep a small pot or bowl near the changing table and bath. Pick him up and hold him over the pot, and happily explain what is happening:

"Mommy's baby is urinating in the pot! Yes! What a champ!"

Again, your actions and tone matter more than your words. If the timing is right so that your baby urinates in his pot many times, and if your smiles and praise let him know that you are pleased, he may figure out what is happening. If you bring him the potty bowl when he has been dry for a while, he may begin pushing to make himself urinate into it.

Happy Students Make Happy Parents

If babies can't walk and toddlers won't slow down, when should you potty train? An ideal time to begin is after babies can sit up by themselves but before they can walk. Once tykes start toddling about on their own, they are constantly on the move, and it is harder to get them to sit still and relax on the potty. If they're already accustomed to the potty when they begin walking, they may be delighted to use their two newly mobile legs to take themselves there.

Introducing the Potty

While carrying your baby to the potty, speak excitedly to communicate that something delightful is about to happen:

"You're going to sit on your potty! Won't that be fun?"

Your tone matters far more than your words, of course. Your exclamations of delight on seeing your little darling sitting on her potty will probably be enough to convince her that she is doing something wonderful. If so, you will likely see a broad smile and excited waving of arms and legs. Add some tickles to get across the message that potty time is fun time.

A Captive Audience

After babies have learned to sit up by themselves and before they learn to walk, two things are certain: babies enjoy playing with the big people in their lives, and babies do not exactly have lots of activities on their agenda. Playing with your baby while he is on the potty can give him a chance for some fun

Mommy Must

Your child must be ready for the baby-track method. She must be able to sit on her own without slouching, listing, tilting, or needing a prop for at least ten minutes. Until then, your baby is too young to sit on the potty!

while accustoming him to sitting bare-bottomed on a chair with a hole. Before babies are mobile, they usually are agreeable to staying put for a few minutes of playtime.

Potty Fear

If your baby is reluctant to try new things, place the potty in his play area for a few days so he can see it. Put a stuffed animal in the bowl and say, "Peek-a-boo!" as you lift it out. After a few days of assorted games, try sitting your child on the potty. The sensation of cold plastic on a bare bottom can be very disconcerting, so leave the diaper on the first few times. Since potty chairs are low to the floor and hot air rises, they are usually much cooler than parents anticipate. If his potty is small enough, it may be possible to sit him on it and hold him on your lap while reading him a story. If he wants to get off, remove him immediately, before he cries or gets upset. One bad experience can take a long time to overcome.

Potty Fun

One characteristic of babies works to your advantage—they love to impress their parents. They adore

Mommy Knows Best

While you dream about diaper-free days, don't forget that being diaper-free is better for your baby, too. Using the potty is far more hygienic than diapers. In fact, it is the best cure for diaper rash. Toxins that leach from disposable diapers and the harsh chemicals used to clean cloth diapers can cause allergic reactions. Potties are healthier!

showing off. If you let your baby know how very cute she is as she sits on her little potty, however briefly, she will soon decide it is a great place to be. If you play pat-a-cake or "So Big," or initiate a Mommy's-gonna-tickle-you game, her staying power may well rival yours.

Babies can have fun engaging in the games parents invent to make sitting on the potty enjoyable. But babies feel overwhelmed and discouraged if parents expect them to fulfill demands they cannot even fathom. Your baby's self-esteem depends on your ability to create reasonable goals. Remember that although it's great if your baby actually uses the potty, the goal is just for him to feel comfortable sitting on it.

- Make sure your baby is seated securely.
- Never leave your baby unattended.
- Keep the tone of every learning session relaxed.
- Remove your baby from the potty the instant she loses interest.
- Do not insist that your baby sit on the potty when she wants off.

Place a blanket or carpet under the potty to prevent a hard bump from an unexpected fall. End each session before your baby fusses so she'll want to sit there again. Consider how hard it is to get toddlers over their potty fears, and you'll realize that just sitting is a giant step!

Once on the Potty

After your baby enjoys rousing games and tickle sessions while sitting on the potty, start teaching him to relax while sitting there. Provide a small toy so he can spend a few moments entertaining himself while you converse quietly or just watch. The long-range goal is for your child to sit quietly for ten or fifteen minutes. It can take several months to get to this point. Even then, never leave him unattended. If he falls, you may be back to square one. If he resists sitting on the potty for whatever reason, don't push. Give him a break for a week or two before trying again.

Establishing Potty Patterns

For the next step, getting your baby to use the potty, you need to recognize her digestive patterns. Pay close attention to her elimination habits so you can anticipate what will be in her diaper when. Many youngsters eliminate like clockwork soon after awakening and about twenty minutes after a meal. If you don't know your child's patterns, remove the diaper for a day so you can see when she relieves herself and carefully record the times.

Be forewarned: This is likely to be a very messy day. Once you get a feel for her patterns, make an effort to put her on her little potty at times she is most likely to need to use it.

Regulating Those Patterns

If your baby sips and snacks all day long, his elimination patterns may be too erratic to predict. You may want to talk to your pediatrician about whether eliminating some snacking might be better for your baby's overall health. Even so, some children's systems are just naturally irregular. In that case, put your baby on the potty after his first morning meal and after naps.

Success!

If you regularly place your youngster on the potty for ten minutes at an expected time of urination or a bowel movement, one or both will eventually occur by coincidence. Given that so many parents have such trouble getting their toddler to sit, this can be seen as a potty training victory!

When your baby uses the potty and you react with enthusiasm, she won't understand what she did that created such excitement and pleased you so. It's like smiling—babies smile accidentally and don't realize

Mindful Mommy

The more enthusiastic you are, the better! If you really ham it up and praise your baby when he uses the potty, he will be encouraged to try to use it the next time you put him on. Some babies respond more enthusiastically to silliness than praise.

they have done something special until you respond with delight. After a few more accidental smiles and enthusiastic responses, babies begin to associate their action (smiling) with their parents' reaction (delight). Eventually, babies smile on purpose in hopes of getting their parents to react.

After your baby makes the association between using the potty and your enthusiastic response, he will automatically push to try to empty his bowel and bladder when you put him on the potty. If anything is in his bowel or bladder, it will come out. You can avoid accidents when you know his patterns and put him onto the potty before urine and stool accumulate to the point that his body automatically expels waste.

How often you can put your baby on the potty will depend on your family schedule. If you work, put him on the potty for a few minutes each morning for a once-a-day practice, and add a second practice after dinner. How soon using the potty becomes a habit depends on how often he sits on it and actually uses it. Putting a baby who is ill on the potty is a bad idea, unless he insists or has trouble bringing himself to go in a diaper.

It does not make sense to put a tired, cranky baby on the potty, either, unless he wants to use it. Your baby's overall health, well-being, and desire to participate should always be the primary considerations.

Speeding Progress

So when you put your child on the potty he usually goes. When babies develop a conditioned response to the potty, they automatically begin to push as soon as their bottoms touch it. They do not decide to push. Their response is involuntary. If your baby is not pushing, it's probably because she's not using it regularly enough, but who cares? If she has a positive attitude toward potties and elimination, is aware of bodily functions, and is gaining lots of experience sitting on the potty, she's way ahead of the game.

Once babies understand the purpose of the potty, they may begin to signal when they need it. Your child may wriggle, his face may flush, or he may make a special cry. After a while, he may turn toward the potty, reach for it, wave, or look at it and fuss, just as he does when he wants a bottle or toy. Watch for a signal and respond immediately.

Cuing Your Baby

Involve you baby by making a special sound to let her know what is happening. It helps your baby learn to use the potty on cue if you make a special sound

Mindful Mommy

It's not the end of the world if you can't get your baby to the potty each time she passes waste. Even if you put her on the potty only once or twice per day, she can learn the purpose of the potty, practice using it, and come to accept the potty as part of the daily routine. That can make training easier during the toddler years.

such as "SSSS" or "SHSHSH" every time she relieves herself, even if she is wetting her diaper or having an accident. She will come to associate the sound you make with elimination. Eventually when you put her on the potty and make the special sound, she will push to try to go. If she actually uses the potty, praise her heartily! She can't use it unless she has waste in her system, so don't be upset if nothing happens. Don't be upset if she has an accident shortly after you take her off the potty, either. Learning takes time.

If your baby acts as if she wants the potty but does not use it, perhaps she wanted to play with it. It's good for her to like her potty, so sanitize it and let her play!

Missed or Confused Signals

When your baby signals for the potty, his need to urinate or have a bowel movement may be imminent, so you must get him to it fast. However, babies often misinterpret their physical sensations. Just as they fail to signal when they need to use the potty, or do not signal in time, they sometimes signal when they don't need it at all. And sometimes, babies need a few minutes so they can relax enough to use it.

Mindful Mommy

You should start to see that your lessons are working within a month or two after you sat her on the potty for the first time if you get her there and she uses it regularly. She should start looking toward it or reaching for it when she wants it. Respond quickly, and praise her lots if she ends up using it. You're getting somewhere!

Even young toddlers who know which muscles to use to "hold it" for a bit may forget to relax them once they are on the potty. If babies try to crawl or walk to the potty by themselves, they may get distracted en route. Even if they go directly to the potty the moment the urge hits, they won't always make it in time. Babies are even less predictable. Expect accidents!

Before potty training, your baby may have slept through the night without a problem. After he starts using the potty, he may awaken and cry during the night because he needs to use it. Anytime a baby who has been using the potty becomes cranky, put him on the potty before trying other ways to calm him.

Oops

As a reflex, your baby may begin urinating or having a bowel movement the moment her diaper is removed instead of waiting to be placed on the potty. Don't scare her as you dive for cover. Avoid any sort of harsh or rough handling, angry words, shouts, or reprimands. Make your special sound, such as "ssss" or "shshsh" whenever and wherever she is relieving herself so she associates elimination with your

Mommy Must

If your baby's stool is looser than normal or he has diarrhea, he may need to wear diapers for a time. Strings of accidents during stressful periods are also to be expected. Sometimes babies simply stage a "potty strike," and parents never do figure out why they suddenly refuse to use it.

sound. In the future, wait to remove the diaper until you have carried her to the potty. Add smiles, nods, and coos of delight when she uses it. Otherwise, just make the special sound while she relieves herself and clean her up without comment. In time, she will be conditioned to wait for the potty.

When They Go on Strike

It is confusing for any parent who thinks they are well on their way and something contrary suddenly happens. A baby who has really been enjoying the potty may suddenly fuss the minute he is placed on it and want to get off. Perhaps last time he fell off and bumped his head, or a sibling burst into the room and startled him. Perhaps he's getting sick. Perhaps he just doesn't feel like it. It doesn't matter why a baby does not want to sit on the potty—it only matters that he doesn't. Remove him!

If your baby is busy playing and refuses to go to the potty, tell him you must put on a diaper so he doesn't make a mess, and change him immediately. Do not be mad if he fusses and cries, but don't let

Mommy Knows Best

It is possible for a potty strike to last a couple of days. If this happens, stop putting him on the potty for a week before trying again. If he still resists, wait a month before reintroducing the potty gradually. Even if he goes many months without using it, you will see during the toddler years that he benefited from his early training.

him continue playing until he's been changed. Let him choose whether he will use the potty right now or put on a diaper right now.

When your baby learns to walk, encourage your young toddler to use the potty by letting him participate in the tasks he enjoys, such as getting toilet paper, wiping himself, emptying the potty bowl, and flushing. Help him with the chores he dislikes, such as dressing and washing his hands.

If you have trained your baby before she can walk, she may have a setback once she does start walking. She may be too excited about exploring to take time out to go to the potty. Be patient! Soon she will be doing both!

A Lesson in Growing Up

Once your baby uses the potty most of the time, she can wear training pants instead of diapers. When she signals that she wants her potty after she has learned to crawl, put it two feet away and call her to it so she can begin learning to crawl toward it when she needs it. That way, when she is walking, she'll know to take herself, though she will still need help with dressing and cleanup. Do not be surprised if you feel you are a slave to your young toddler's bowel and bladder. You'll still have to help your child remove her clothes, wipe herself, put her clothes back on, empty the potty bowl into the toilet, flush, and wash her hands until she's old enough to handle everything herself. Your job as a parent is far from done!

Chapter 5

How Can We Practice?
Potty Practice Method

THE POTTY PRACTICE METHOD is the traditional way to train toddlers. As a potty coach, you will matter-of-factly introduce your child to the potty and teach each step of the mechanics of how to use it. To be successful, this method requires getting your child to the potty at times he needs to use it and teaching him to sit still and relax enough so that he actually can go. At the outset, getting little wigglers to stay put can be the hardest part!

Schedules and Flexibility Go Hand-in-Hand

Practice makes perfect! You can use this method if your toddler is eighteen months or older, and after teaching the readiness skills that were discussed earlier in this book. You will gradually introduce the potty, present basic lessons about bowel movements and urination, and hold regular potty practice sessions. During potty practice sessions have your child sit on the potty at scheduled times. Have him handle assorted chores, such as undressing, wiping, dressing, removing the potty bowl, emptying it into the toilet, flushing, replacing the potty bowl, washing hands, etc., as much as possible. Because potty practice sessions can be arranged to fit busy schedules, this method is workable for most families. Most of the time is spent on the area toddlers find most challenging: sitting still and relaxing.

Scheduled Practices Are Important

Although many modern families are continually rushed and lack fixed daily schedules, it will help your toddler if you follow a routine. Holding regularly scheduled potty practices can seem a bit taxing at times. But a schedule helps regulate your child's system. Try to have your child eat, nap, exercise, sleep, and use the potty at the same times every day. You could end up with not only a potty-trained child, but also a calmer, happier family.

Because every child is different, you should adapt this method to your child's needs. If your child catches on quickly and is highly self-motivated,

Mommy Must

Try to hold potty practices when your child might need to use the potty. Most toddlers urinate shortly after awakening and about twenty minutes after eating or drinking. Otherwise, they urinate about once every two hours.

there is no need to continue to require lots of potty practices. Consider switching to the potties-without-pressure method, or try some of the techniques from the fast-track toddler method described later.

What to Expect as a Coach

If your eighteen-month-old finishes training fast, he will probably continue to need help with clothing for quite some time. He may continue to have an occasional accident when his timing is off or he struggles to remove his clothing. You must continue to supervise unless your bathroom has been thoroughly baby-proofed. Have your child use a potty chair instead of a potty seat so that the regular toilet can remain locked.

How Long Will It Take?

There are a number of factors that determine how quickly your child will finish training, namely the frequency of the practice sessions and his maturity, temperament, and motivation. Frequent practices can speed learning. However, working parents often find this method works well, even though they can only get their child onto the potty a couple of times a day on weekdays. There is no way to guess how long it will take for potty practice sessions to work their magic. Some children are still learning to remain seated and sit still long enough to have a chance to use the potty while others have finished training.

Stress May Cause Setbacks

If your tot suddenly refuses to go near their potty, don't take it personally. It is a mistake to assume he is punishing you or trying to make you miserable. If you feel frustrated by slow progress or setbacks, that doesn't mean your child is trying to upset you! Even after toddlers finish potty training, they may have setbacks. During a particularly difficult period, they may regress, have a string of accidents, or refuse to use the potty altogether, so that they must return to diapers or wear pull-ups for a time. The stress can be due to something in the child's environment—perhaps a change in day care teachers or a divorce.

Stress can also be due to what is happening within the child. During that terribly-two-year-old stage when toddlers' desire to be all grown up and in control collides with the reality of being young and helpless, potty refusals and accidents can become real problems. Fortunately, once your child is back on an even keel, returning to frequent practice sessions can be accomplished in short order. In the meantime:

Mommy Knows Best

You can avoid tantrums and guilty feelings if you use an egg timer to signal the beginning and ending of potty practice sessions. A timer helps focus your child's upset about having to sit on the potty away from you. Let it be the timer's fault that he has to practice for a few minutes. The egg timer never gets offended, and can take the heat!

- Continue taking your child into the bathroom regularly even if he won't sit on the potty.
- Take a book for him to read or something to occupy him. Studiously ignore tantrums, but make sure he doesn't hurt himself by throwing himself about.
- Once he learns that he must remain in the bathroom until he's calmed down, his tantrums will subside.
- Soon after he's stopped struggling and remains calm, he'll be willing to sit the potty for a bit.
- When he relaxes, he'll be able to use the potty if the timing of the practice sessions is right.

Trouble with the Next Step

A potential problem of the potty practice method is that some children get to the point of being virtually accident-free because they use the potty whenever their parent initiates a practice session at the right time. Nevertheless, they have trouble taking the next step: figuring out when they need to use the potty on their own and going without being prompted. They can seem quite stuck for a while. If so, the motivational tricks and tactics described at the end of the chapter can help them complete training, as can the accident management strategies described later on in the book.

How to Get Started with This Method

Use a potty chair rather than a potty seat. Tell your toddler that it is his, and set it in the play area so he can get used to it. Be sure that your child's bottom is covered the first few times he sits on it—the cold plastic can be so off-putting that some youngsters determine to make that first unpleasant surprise their last.

If your child wants to sit on his potty bare-bottomed right away, suggest he touch the seat with his hands to test the temperature. If he thinks it is cold, the two of you can warm it with your hands for a minute first. First impressions are especially important for very timid, sensitive toddlers. Do what you can to make them good ones.

Keep the potty chair in the living room or your child's bedroom until he is comfortable with it, and then start storing it in the bathroom. You can still let him take it out and play with it, if you are comfortable with him using it as a toy.

Mommy Must

After your child relieves himself in his potty, sanitize it by wiping it down with a mild bleach solution before letting him play with it. To teach your child how to wipe himself correctly after using the potty, see the hygiene section in this book.

Demonstrating

For the first potty practice sessions, have your child accompany you to the bathroom while you use the toilet. The goals are for your child to get comfortable being in the bathroom for five or ten minutes, and to begin learning the process by watching you. It helps to pull down your underwear and actually use it. If that is too uncomfortable for you, at least lift the lid, sit down, and pretend. If your child senses your discomfort, he may conclude something scary is about to happen and feel afraid, so try to relax. Calmly explain,

"Mommy is sitting on her big toilet. The potty is your little toilet."

Take a book or magazine with you. Spend a few minutes reading, and suggest your child do the same. Stay relaxed so she can see that bathrooms and potties are nothing to be worried about.

It's fine if your child wants to sit on his potty, but wait a few days until the novelty of being with you in the bathroom has worn off before suggesting it. If he sits on it with his clothes on, just say,

"You're sitting on your little potty. Are you going to urinate or have a B.M.?"

If he pretends to use it standing up "like Dad," explain that little boys have to sit down until they learn how. Nevertheless, don't squelch his desire to experiment. Let him take his time and get comfortable with the situation.

If Your Child Isn't Interested

If your child isn't interested in sitting on the potty after she has accompanied you to the bathroom several times, suggest that her doll or stuffed animal might want to go potty. Take a book or magazine with you and spend a few minutes reading and suggest she do the same. Stay relaxed so she can see that bathrooms and potties are nothing to be worried about. Spend a few minutes in the bathroom each day for a week before suggesting she sit on the potty bare-bottomed. Tell her to touch the potty seat first to make sure it isn't cold. Use your hands to warm the seat, and suggest she help you. Plan to move very slowly. In the end, you'll be glad you did!

If your child's reluctance to sit on the potty continues, she may have already absorbed some negative attitudes toward passing waste, be worried about what is expected of her, or be especially active or immature. Try taking the potty to the living room for potty practice. Have her sit on it fully clothed while you read her a story so she can start getting used to

Mommy Knows Best

It helps if the same-sexed parent or older sibling can serve as a role model. It helps, too, if little boys can see an older male sit down to use the toilet as well as use it while standing.

sitting on it. Push it up to the coffee table and let her sit on it to eat a picnic lunch in the living room. See if she wants to sit on it bare-bottomed while you work a puzzle together.

Teaching about Bowel Movements

If the idea of using the bathroom with your child present makes you too uncomfortable, invite him in after you have used it. In either case, point to your B.M. in the toilet and explain that it is "Mommy's B.M." or whatever word he is to use. After he is tired of looking at it, encourage him to wave and tell it "bye-bye" as you flush. Tell him that your body makes a B.M. every day and that you will show him again tomorrow. Encourage him to sit on his potty to see if he can make a B.M., too. If he brings up the subject of "Mommy's B.M." later in the day, keep a stiff upper lip even if it embarrasses you. Repeat the same procedure during a potty practice every day for about a week.

Meanwhile, whenever you notice that your child is having a B.M., bring it to his attention. As soon as he is finished, take him to the bathroom to remove his soiled diapers. Scrape the stool into the toilet while he watches, saying,

"I'm putting your B.M. in the toilet just like Mommy's."

When he is tired of looking at it, see if he wants to flush. Some youngsters become upset about their bowel movements being disposed of, as if a part of themselves were being flushed away. To try to stave off upset, wave bye-bye together, and explain that flushing is so:

"Our B.M.s can be together."

Tell him you'll put your B.M.s in the toilet again as soon as your body makes more, and that his B.M.s will go in the toilet as soon as his body makes more. If he doesn't want to wave good-bye or looks even a little bit concerned, close the lid and wait to flush until he leaves the room. The point is to try to stave off the intense "separation anxiety" so many toddlers develop. Many youngsters become so upset about their bowel movements being disposed of, they refuse to have a B.M. in the potty.

Teaching about Urination

Let your child accompany you to the bathroom for potty practice several days in a row and have her listen for when "Mommy is putting her urine in the toilet" or watch Daddy putting his in. Explain, "I am making urine now," in case she doesn't notice the sound. Explain:

"You put your urine in your diaper. Soon you will put it in the potty like me."

Repeat the explanation whenever you discover a wet diaper. Be enthusiastic as you say,

"They're wet because you put your urine in your diaper. Where does Mommy put hers? Yes! In her big potty! Where will you put yours someday? Yes! In your little potty," or some such.

The goal is to help her to understand the basics of urination, that big people use the toilet, and that some day she will use it, too.

To show your child how urination works, feed water to a doll that wets and hold it over the toilet so your child can watch it urinate in the toilet. Give the doll another bottle and have her hold the doll over her potty, or hold it for her. Explain that she will use her potty like the doll. Then make a tissue-paper diaper and put it on the doll with tape. Feed it another bottle, make it wet, and have your child feel its diaper as you explain, "It went pee-pee in its diaper." Later, when your child is drinking liquid, tell her that she will urinate soon. Just like the doll, she will wet her diaper. Explain that someday she will put her urine in her little potty like Mommy puts hers in her big potty.

Mindful Mommy

Since birth, your toddler has relieved himself automatically. Diapers hid the connection between sensations of fullness, and of wetting and soiling. He will need to see himself eliminating to grasp what is happening. Remove the diaper and prepare for a messy day!

Ask Your Child to Notify You

When your child is drinking, remind her about the doll that wets. Tell her that because she is drinking, she will soon wet her diaper like her doll. Ask her to tell you when that happens. From time to time, ask,

"Did the urine come yet?"

If she says it did, check her diaper. If she is correct, exclaim,

"Yes! Your urine came! You put it in your diaper!"

Be very happy indeed, if she can actually tell when she is urinating. If she was wrong, consider that disposable diapers mask the sensations to the point that she can't tell what's going on. Switch to cloth diapers so she can feel the wetness.

Ask your child often to tell you when her urine is coming, but if she doesn't like to have her diaper changed, postpone changing her. You want her to notice when "the urine is coming," not ignore it because she doesn't like being changed. If she tells you it is coming and her diaper is dry, say,

"No, not yet. But soon it will come."

Prepotty Practice

After watching your child carefully and noting the times at which he eats and eliminates on a calendar, schedule one or more daily potty practices when your child is likely to have a bowel movement. Some children regularly have a bowel movement a half hour or so after a big meal, regardless of when they eat.

Several Daily Practices

Only hold one practice a day until your child willingly stays in the bathroom for five minutes and sits on the potty for at least a minute without a struggle. Then, if your schedule permits, hold a daily potty practice when you expect your child to have a bowel movement. If she is too irregular to predict, set up a schedule and hold a potty practice:

- First thing in the morning
- Shortly after breakfast
- Midmorning or immediately after a morning nap
- Shortly after lunch

Mommy Must

Punishing accidents by leaving your child in wet or messy clothes is abusive. The risk of rash and infection increases. In addition, he may become accustomed to wet diapers, so your punishment will backfire. Instead, have your child bathe and help wipe up puddles.

- Midafternoon or immediately after her afternoon nap
- Shortly after dinner
- Before bed

Although you should try to schedule practices for bowel movements, more frequent sessions give your child more opportunities to urinate in the potty. Busy dual-income families and single working parents can ask day care providers to have their youngster spend five minutes in the bathroom at likely times or at regular intervals. Alternatively, hold potty practices once or twice a day on workdays and more often on the weekends.

Do Your Best

If family schedules and unreliable caregivers make several daily practices impossible, have your child practice first thing in the morning and after breakfast. Pick a time or two in the evening, perhaps after dinner and just before bed.

If you can only manage one or two daily practices during the work week, toddlers can learn to remain seated, relax, and use the potty. However, it may take

Mindful Mommy

Being able to use the potty isn't just a question of sitting on it at the right time. Children must have waste in their systems, and they must be relaxed enough for their sphincters to open up so the waste can flow out.

them much longer to develop the habit of going to the potty each and every time they need to relieve themselves. Try putting the potty chair in the living room so your child can sit on it while he is playing at a small desk, watching a video, or listening to a story. Have him wear pull-ups so he can easily use the potty any time he wants to. And be sure to provide a reward whenever he does use it. It may be necessary to finish potty training during a weeklong stay-at-home vacation so you can hold practices once every two hours.

Start on the Right Foot

When your child doesn't object to sitting on the potty without a diaper, begin generating excitement for the big event. Announce that he will wear pull-ups and learn to use the potty just like Mommy/Daddy/big brother/big sister and all the big kids at day care. Choose a time when he is in a good mood, rested, and healthy.

Take him to the bathroom shortly before you expect him to have a bowel movement and close the door. Put a small piece of toilet paper in the potty so that if he urinates just a tiny bit, you will be able to tell by looking at the paper and can congratulate him. Show him how to pull his pants and pull-ups down to his ankles, bending at the knees so he doesn't fall. Have him sit all the way back on the potty chair with the legs slightly spread so you can see and point out what is happening if he begins urinating.

If He Wants to Stand

If your child wants to use the potty standing up, explain that big boys and Daddies sit to have B.M.s and stand to urinate, and that he can stand, too, after he learns to use it sitting down. Don't press him, though. He is likely to be more excited than usual, which may make sitting extra hard. Encourage him to focus on his physical sensations by telling him to let you know when he feels like his urine or B.M. wants to come out. Children also urinate when they have bowel movements, so if a bowel movement starts, tell him to sit on the potty fast and hold his penis down. However, moving too fast could cause him to bump a splashguard, which hurts. Remove it to guard against a painful accident.

Helping Your Child

Show your child how to "try" to have a bowel movement by grunting and acting as if you're straining. However, many toddlers tense their sphincter muscles in the process, so "trying" may not work. To stimulate urination, run some water in the sink or dip his hands in a bowl of tepid water. Researchers say that is just an old wives' tale, but lots of old wives

Mindful Mommy

Time potty practice sessions to coincide with expected bowel movements. Urine is passed when children have a B.M. Hence, as they use the potty for bowel movements, they practice urinating in the potty, too.

say it works! Teach your child to relax by closing your eyes, taking slow, deep breaths, and telling him to do the same. If he wanders, tell him to stay near the potty so he can sit down when he needs to use it. Don't press him to remain seated—he may be too tense to relieve himself anyway.

First Success

If your child begins eliminating unexpectedly when he isn't sitting on the potty, tell him to try to stop. Few toddlers know how to stop once they've started, but at least he'll know it's possible, and it's important to start teaching the lesson that he should go to the potty whenever he is passing waste. If he does stop, say, "Good boy!" and guide him to the potty fast.

Have an extra bowl within easy reach so that if he has the usual toddler reaction of standing still and watching himself urinate, you can try to catch some urine in the extra bowl and pour it into his potty bowl to show him where it's supposed to go. If you can't catch any in a bowl, get a very wet sponge or soaking wet washcloth when he finishes urinating, wipe up some urine with the sponge, and squeeze some into his potty. Be enthusiastic as you say something like,

Mommy Must

End each potty session by having your child wash his hands whether or not he used the potty. This is the way to start developing the hand-washing habit!

"Your urine came out and I'm putting it in the potty where it belongs!"

When he is through admiring it, help him pour the contents of the potty bowl into the toilet,

"So it can go bye-bye with Mama's urine"

Invite him to flush, but if he doesn't respond, flush after he has left the room. The violence of the swirling water upsets many children.

On the Right Track

Your child has now been through the entire process and should have a better idea as to what's involved even if he didn't have a bowel movement or urinate in the potty. Hold practice sessions regularly, about once every two hours, and try to have him sit on the potty for five minutes each time.

When he notifies you that he needs to use the potty or takes himself, you may not need to hold regular practice sessions. Help him share the good news that he's starting to learn to use the potty with a friend or family member. He's earned his bragging rights!

Mommy Must

Until using the potty has become a habit, your child must constantly keep tabs on the fullness of her bladder and bowel. Such extended concentration is exhausting. Don't be surprised if she is especially cranky and tired. Scale back your expectations in other areas, and pour on the TLC.

If Nothing Happens

If your child doesn't urinate or have a bowel movement during his first potty practice session, he either didn't need to use it or was too tense to release waste. Begin holding regular potty practice sessions timed to coincide with when you expect he might need to go. For each session, have him spend three to five minutes practicing sitting on his potty and relaxing. Insist that he stay in the bathroom; encourage him to remain seated. If he protests strongly, remain calm and let the tantrum run its course—which may mean you end up in the bathroom for a very long time. Don't have a tantrum, too, by yelling or getting upset. Simply keep him with you in the bathroom until he is completely calm (unless you're losing it and need a break) so you can end each upsetting session on a positive note:

"You calmed down!"

Give him the rest of the day to recover rather than holding another potty practice session. After two or three tantrums, your child should understand that lots of noisy upset won't induce you to end a potty practice session early. Then, it should get easier.

Even if your timing is good and your child remains seated on the potty during the practices, he may still be too tense to eliminate. Don't be surprised if he soils or wets as soon as he stands up, or shortly after the practice session ends and his diaper is back on. This is normal. The sphincter stays closed when he's tense and opens when he relaxes. Tell him he can try again later. Wait about two hours, and hold another potty practice. Devote the sessions to helping him relax until he can comfortably remain seated for five minutes.

If your child uses the potty, have her empty and rinse the potty bowl, and wash her hands. If she has an accident shortly before a practice session, hold it anyway if you think she would benefit from practicing sitting on the potty and relaxing.

Relaxation Training

When your child has a potty practice session, remind her that she must relax so that she can use the potty. Keep your focus positive by noting anything she does right as she works on relaxing:

"Your arms are resting now. That's a good way to relax," or *"You're sitting nicely."*

If she swings her legs, wait until she stops swinging them and then tell her that you're glad she's holding them still. Show her how to relax while sitting on

Mommy Knows Best

Show your toddler boy how to hold his penis down to direct the stream of urine. Help him remember to concentrate by giving positive feedback: "You're getting the urine in the potty! Very good!" When he forgets, give him a sponge to help clean up, and give him positive feedback: "Great! You're cleaning the splashes!"

the potty by closing your eyes and breathing deeply as you sit on the toilet.

Put your arm on her fidgety hands to show her how to hold still, and say, "Yes! That's the way to sit still." It may be tempting to strap your little busy bee to the potty chair to keep her there, but that is abusive! Keeping her in wet or soiled pants as punishment teaches nothing and is abusive, too.

Another way to help your child relax is to make the time pleasant. Sit next to her on the floor while she sits on the potty and read her a book, sing a song together, or recite nursery rhymes. Avoid rowdy play. Eventually you want her to sit by herself without needing to be entertained, but distracting her at the outset with a book or quiet game will help her relax. Children have a hard time relaxing and sitting still if they have a lot of pent-up energy. Provide time for active play before each potty practice session.

Clothing

It's generally too messy to let children wear underpants until they use the potty at least half of the time, but the problem with diapers is that children can't get them off easily to use the potty by themselves. By having your child put on pull-ups or underpants for each potty practice, she can practice pulling them down before sitting on the potty and pulling them back up at the end of the session. You can then put on her diaper before sending her off to play. However, some toddlers can more easily remember to go to the potty when wearing cloth pull-ups or underpants because they are so aware of being in big-girl clothes. By wearing cloth, they can immediately tell when they've had an accident, so after an accident or two many children learn to get themselves to the potty in time. It's worth a try. If your child is having too many accidents to make it practical for her to wear underpants outside of potty practice sessions, you can solve the problem by putting her in diapers or covering her underpants with a waterproof cover. A compromise for a child who insists on wearing underpants is to let her wear them as long as she keeps them clean and dry. Put her in diapers after each accident, and then reward her for using the potty by letting her change into underpants afterward.

Small Rewards

Small rewards help motivate children to remain seated, provided that the rewards are easy for them to earn. Set up your youngster to succeed, never to fail. Give a sticker for staying seated for just one or two minutes at first, and slowly work up to five minutes. Only reward real successes. Don't break down and give her a reward because she's sad, but the accomplishments can be very small ones.

Mommy Must

Have your child prepare for potty practice by dancing, running, or engaging in other vigorous play to work off energy. To boost motivation to practice and lessen tot's resistance to sitting on the potty, provide a special toy or book that invites quiet, relaxed play and designate it for use during potty practice sessions only.

Track Progress

Once your child can relax on the potty, he should be able to have bowel movements during potty practice if your timing is right. With more frequent practices timed to his patterns of urinating, he should be able to make rapid progress. Track his progress on a calendar or chart by noting the times he uses the potty, and have him affix a sticker as a reward. You might provide a very special sticker each time he goes to the potty outside of a scheduled session, too. Write down the time of each accident so you can do a better job of scheduling his practice sessions.

Who's the Boss?

Be sure your child understands that if he goes potty by himself, he won't need his regular potty practice session. Then, when the scheduled time for a practice session has arrived, reinforce his accomplishment by announcing:

"It's time for potty practice, but you went potty by yourself so you can keep on playing. You don't need to practice."

A Common Problem

Some children become very good at using the potty during regularly scheduled practice sessions. The problem is, they only use it when their parent takes them to the bathroom. Otherwise, they go in their pants. Suggestions that they take themselves when they need to go potty seem to fall on deaf ears. Don't think your child is being defiant! The sensation of a diaper, pull-ups, or underwear triggers the old habit of passing waste. After each accident they may feel very repentant but not improve.

A Solution

Some children have difficulty connecting the sensations of a full bladder or bowel with the waste that flows from the body. One solution is to have your child go bare-bottomed for a day to help her comprehend this all-important connection. Keep the potty close by and see if she can use it without having to be told. Ask:

"Do you need to use the potty?"

Even if you see signs that she needs to relieve herself, don't press her to sit on it. Her first response may well be to have an accident. If so, she probably hasn't made the connection between the sensations of

Mommy Knows Best

If your child complies with potty practice rules but won't go to the potty on his own, try the Tickle Game or Beat the Clock explained later. These games will help him understand what you expect and will encourage him to take the initiative.

fullness and passing waste. Tell her to run to the potty the next time she feels:

"The urine or B.M. wanting to come."

Repeat this procedure as often as necessary so she can learn to make the connection. Continue to encourage her to sit on the potty when she feels her urine coming.

In the meantime, give her a sponge so she can start learning to clean up, but don't insist that she actually do any work. If she does go potty by herself or asks to be taken even once as her day of going bare-bottomed wears on, this could be a major turning point. Be enthusiastic and reward her. Try to keep her pants off for the rest of the day, and let her go bare-bottomed for the next few days to help the habit develop of going to the potty each and every time.

Reconditioning

If your child continues to have one accident after the next while she is bare-bottomed, don't assume the problem is lack of motivation. Many parents condition their babies only to relieve themselves when their bottoms are covered. You may have done this by shrieking when you were unexpectedly sprayed while changing a diaper, or by yelling for your baby to stop urinating when her diaper was off. If a baby is startled by the parent's shrieks and yells, the sphincter may clamp shut. When urination stops, the upsetting noise the parent was making stops, too.

Afterward, whenever the baby's bottom is bare, the sphincters tighten to contain waste inside the body in order to prevent any more of those startling shrieks and yells. The sphincters only relax enough for waste to be released in two situations: when the diaper or underpants are on, or when the pressure of an overly full bladder and/or bowel suddenly forces them open. The result is lots of accidents.

The solution to having to have the bottom covered to eliminate is to recondition the sphincters. The following tricks and tactics can help.

Tactics, Tricks, and Techniques

It's amazing how a single trick can capture toddlers' imagination and provide a permanent motivational fix. In addition, these tactics can help recondition the sphincters so they can open instead of remaining closed as long as possible whenever your child's bottom is bare.

Sail the ping-pong ball. Drop a ping-pong ball in the toilet bowl and let toddler boys sail it with their

Mommy Knows Best

Recondition sphincters that have been conditioned to remain shut whenever your child's bottom is bare by creating a distraction to "confuse" them. Do that by singing or playing with him while he is sitting on the potty.

spray. This will help them learn to aim. Wash your hands after retrieving the ball!

Bull's eye. Draw a magic marker target on a piece of tissue paper, and drop it in the potty or toilet bowl. See if your little boy can score a hit. Your little girl may get a kick out of this kind of target practice, too, even if she can't see what she's doing.

Sink or swim? Float a piece of paper towel in the toilet bowl and see if your toddler can sink it. Improve his aim by using progressively smaller pieces.

Firefighter. Suggest your toddler don his firefighter hat and douse the imaginary blaze raging in the toilet with his urine. That means, of course, that he will have to go fast if he's to save the house from ruin. Next time he's wiggling because he needs to use the potty, don't yell, "Go to the potty now!" Just yell, "Fire!"

Gardener. Paint flowers inside the potty bowl or affix stickers featuring flowers. Alternatively, cut the flower designs from printed paper towels and drop them into the toilet. Then, declare the "garden" in need of a sprinkle. If it's time to have a bowel movement, what the heck? Suggest the flowers need to be fertilized!

Sweeter than roses. Tell your child how nice she smells now that she's used the potty and kept her pants clean. To drive home the message, squirt her with a dollop of cologne. Little boys love this, too.

Meet the Lump family. Are her B.M.s big enough to be the "daddies," small enough to be the "children," or the right size to count as "mommies"?

Have her decide. Then she can tuck them in for the night by flushing.

Toilet rainbows. Add a few drops of blue food coloring in the toilet bowl (or a bit of water and food coloring to the potty bowl) so your child can delight in watching it turn green when he adds yellow urine. Or, color the water red so he can turn it orange.

Bare-bottomed. Underpants feel enough like diapers to some children that they forget they're wearing them. The old habit kicks in and they do what they've done since the day they were born: relieve themselves without pausing to consider. Remove their underwear, and the strange sensation of nakedness serves as an on-going reminder to use the potty, even if they are still wearing a dress or pants. After a few days of constant awareness, they can wear underwear again without forgetting.

High fashion. The chance to don special "big boy" or "big girl" pull-ups or underpants can be exciting. The downside is that accidents can be very messy and require a complete change of clothes. Encourage your child to concentrate by setting the rule up front: "You can wear your underpants when you're ready to use the potty." Place them out of reach but within view, such as on top of a dresser, and wait for your child to ask to wear them. Alternatively, offer them as a reward: Every time your child uses the potty, she can wear them until she has an accident.

Big is better! Rewards must be immediate to be effective, but sometimes the visual reward of a check mark or sticker on a calendar for each dry day is a potent incentive—especially if a week's worth of checks can be exchanged for a very special toy or outing. Thinking so far ahead may be beyond most toddlers, but one four-year-old stayed dry from the day his parents promised to buy the antique Civil War sword he was determined to have decorating the wall of his bedroom. Another child went the distance for a Michael Jackson CD. Inappropriate toddler rewards? Perhaps, but what the heck? They worked.

Here, there, and (almost) everywhere! Have your child experiment with urinating in interesting containers—a bucket, jar, tin can, cup, pan, bowl, flowerpot, hole in the ground, etc. This is a great potty training tension reliever, and can help youngsters overcome the idea that the one and only place to urinate is at home in their very own potty. Public restrooms may then be okay, too.

Move it! Nowhere is it written that a child must go to the potty. The potty can just as easily go to your child. Suggest he move it into the play area, put it in his bedroom at night, and set it in the kitchen during meals. Once he gets in the habit of seeking it out when he needs it, you can store it in the bathroom and those few extra steps won't be such a bother. In a carpeted room, try putting a pet pad under the potty chair to help soak up spills and splashes.

The easy chair. Some potties are especially comfy. They have soft seats, tall backs, and arm rests. Why not move your child's potty into the living room so he can relax on it while watching TV? Of course, TV-watching isn't good for toddlers, and they're never supposed to do it. But if they are, maybe they can sit on the potty with their pants down and the lid up and reap a small benefit.

Incentives

It's no wonder so many children have problems staying motivated. When they use the potty, parents reap the rewards, not children. Little ones lose the special one-on-one time they enjoyed during diaper changes. They trade the carefree days of diapers for having to monitor the state of their bladder and bowel at every moment. They have to drop what they're doing and run to the potty time and again. Small presents, hugs, and affection can help encourage your child to work on a task that doesn't seem to him to be worthwhile. The challenge is to keep his motivation high enough for long enough so that the habit of using the

Mindful Mommy

Although it's preferable to have children strive to please parents rather than obtain treats and goodies, the mere act of handing over a reward helps parents to stay involved and express approval with their actions, if not their words.

potty can be established. When going potty becomes second nature, he won't have to work so hard. In the meantime, rewards can also keep the tone of potty training positive and upbeat.

Sweet Rewards

Candy is not the sort of reward health-conscious parents want to give, but it may be the best way to motivate your child. If stickers and small toys don't work or are too expensive, try for something like a raisin, fish cracker, or tidbit of whole grain cereal before moving to a small piece of candy or tidbit of sugary cereal. Dole one out each time your child uses the potty or completes a specific task that is giving him problems, such as going to the potty without a prompt or reminder, wiping himself after bowel movements, aiming, wiping splashes from the sink after hand washing, or flushing the toilet.

If your child has really big problems with one particular task, provide a more enticing reward to help him focus and motivate him to struggle on. For instance, if he sometimes gets himself to the potty to urinate but never for a B.M., give one piece for the former and buy him a Porsche for the latter. Well,

Mommy Knows Best

If your child does not care about praise or rewards and you are worried that something is wrong, don't fret. Potty training probably feels far too overwhelming. Try quitting for a month, and start over more gradually. To do that, reward even tiny successes.

maybe just a replica. Be sure to supply other caregivers with stocks of rewards, coordinate so you're on the same page, keep each other informed of progress and problems, and discuss changes in your methods in advance.

Consistency

Too many changes in reward systems can confuse kiddies, so try to think things through in advance. Clearly communicate what your child must do to earn a reward, and exactly what the reward will be. Consider carefully what will count as a success. Sitting still for three minutes? Going to the potty with or without a reminder? Urinating in the potty? Will you set a timer and reward him for every hour that he keeps his diapers dry? If so, that could add up to a lot of M&Ms! Nevertheless, rewarding children for staying clean and dry is definitely a good idea.

It's okay to gradually increase the requirements for earning a reward. For instance, after your toddler is urinating and having B.M.s in the potty without a problem, the next step might be teaching responsibility. In that case, you might require him to complete all toileting tasks to receive a reward:

- Empty the potty bowl
- Flush the toilet
- Dispose of toilet paper scraps
- Wipe up splashes
- Wash and dry hands, etc.

Reward programs bog down when the rules keep changing or are overly complicated: No more candy for urinating in the potty, only a sticker; candy is only for a B.M. but you can have two pieces instead of one, and if you sit still you get a penny. Don't focus on more than two issues at a time, and even that may be too much. Test your child's understanding: "What do you get for urinating in the potty?" and "What do you get for sitting on the potty when a B.M. is coming?" If he can't answer, your reward system may not mean anything to him.

For starters, keep the bag of M&Ms (or whatever) close to the potty but out of reach, accompany your child to the bathroom, and give food rewards by popping them right into his mouth and letting him know what he did right. Otherwise, hand him his food reward when he has finished wiping and flushing and, most importantly, washing his hands. He should never touch food after using the bathroom until his hands are washed.

Gradually separate the candy from the praise by confining yourself to saying what he did right as you give him the reward. Choose other times to mention how pleased you are with the way he's been handling the potty. A good time to make a positive comment might be when you think that he needs to use the potty but isn't moving in that direction:

"You've been so good about going to the potty! You haven't had an accident all day."

If he doesn't respond to your prompt, let the accident happen. He won't learn to take responsibility if you take it for him! Afterward, let him help clean up while you figure out where to get the money for new carpeting when he is finally trained.

Taking More Responsibility

Let your child gradually take more responsibility by giving less direction and fewer prompts as to what to do next. Instead of standing over him to tell him what to do next in the bathroom, wait until he considers himself finished, and then tell him what still needs to be done. After he empties the potty bowl, flushes the toilet, and wipes up splashes from the floor, have him rewash his hands before giving the reward.

Phasing Out Rewards

While parents are usually careful to praise and reward first potty successes, their enthusiasm typically wanes long before children achieve that all-important goal of going to the potty each and every time they need to. Parents tire of having to drop what they are doing to "watch me go!" or "see what I did!" They make excuses so as not to have to participate and become lackadaisical as they distractedly mutter, "That's great." Soon their own disinterest is reflected in their child's waning attention to remaining accident-free. He's as unenthusiastic about going to the potty as the parent is about helping him.

The solution is to remain involved as long as your child needs encouragement to keep going, then phase out your involvement gradually, but only after he is fully trained.

1. Stay with your child in the bathroom the whole time and give him a reward.
2. Help your child get started in the bathroom, leave, go back in, and give him a reward.
3. Tell your child to go to the potty, join him in the bathroom a minute later, and give him a reward.
4. Tell your child to call you when he's finished in the bathroom, join him for a bathroom inspection, check his hands, and give him a reward.
5. Tell your child to come find you when he's finished in the bathroom, check his hands, and then give him a reward.

When your child uses the potty regularly for a week without prompts or reminders, move the rewards to the kitchen. Have him go to the potty by himself and come to you afterward to collect. Check his hands. If they're not clean, send him back to rewash. Check them again when he returns, then give him his due.

The first time your child forgets to ask for his reward, you'll know he's nearing the finish line. Most children then forget to ask with increasing frequency. You can "help" by conversing on another subject after she emerges from the bathroom to distract her. But if she does ask for it, give it immediately! A deal's a deal!

Try offering a choice in hopes of being able to provide rewards you feel better about giving: An

M&M or a sticker? An M&M or a story? An M&M or a trip to the park? An M&M or a trip to the store after lunch to buy new underwear? An M&M or a ride on the mechanical horse at the grocery store? An M&M or a chance to finger paint later in the day? To earn a delayed reward, add that she must not wet or soil beforehand or the deal is off.

M&Ms Forever

When it comes to potty training, parents tend to imagine the worst. Many fear they'll be doling out M&Ms and stickers forever. It just doesn't work out that way. Nevertheless, if your child has been fully trained for quite some time but isn't about to forget to collect his piece of candy after every success, it's time for the healthy teeth cure: Since candy is bad for his teeth, he must brush every time after eating his M&M. If he's willing to brush after each sweet reward, so be it. Don't expect a toddler to do a good job of brushing, but do expect him to put forth a real effort.

Finally, cut out other desserts, snacks, and sodas to balance his diet. A small daily dose of M&Ms is a bargain if it buys a potty-trained child who brushes his teeth six or seven times a day!

Mindful Mommy

When toddlers have mixed feelings about independence, praise can increase power struggles. Instead of trying to get a surly rebel to "do it for Mom," let him just do it for the reward.

Chapter 6

Is There a Faster Way? Fast-Track Toddler Method

THIS METHOD CAN BE fast and painless, but it is an intensive approach. Some children might not react well to it. Also, you must make sure your little one is ready for this method! Given that your child is doing in a day what many toddlers take months to accomplish, be sure you child has the physical, cognitive, emotional, and social skills to succeed before you try. Be sure that you can remain calm, too. A bad potty training experience can take a long time to overcome.

One-Day Training, It's True!

If you have a mature toddler, and your family is pressed for time, the fast-track method might be perfect for you. Children who are twenty months and older can be potty trained with amazing speed. The method for toilet training in less than a day developed by Nathan Azrin and Richard Foxx and described in their book, *Toilet Training in Less Than a Day*, has become a classic. This fast-track method has a number of components.

- Feed your child lots of liquids so she can practice using the potty often during a short period.
- Demonstrate the process using a doll that wets.
- Manually guide your child to ensure she understands and follows directions.
- Teach self-affirmations to instill confidence and boost motivation.
- Give drinks and snacks as rewards to increase urination and boost motivation.
- Have your child practice going to the potty after accidents, so she learns to go without delay when the need arises in the future.

Mixed Reactions

While some parents swear by this method, others think it is much too hard on children and can be harmful. Lots of parents find it easy and enjoyable, and have had success with it after other methods failed. Many parents find the process considerably more challenging, but are still delighted with the speedy results. However, some parents reported that their children became so upset, they had to abandon potty training altogether and wait a month before starting over with a different method. Do not hesitate to stop if you think it is too trying!

It's Not for Everyone

Do you use "time out" to discipline your child? If you do, you may find this fast-track method is out of step with your usual approach to dealing with your child's upset. Many parents consider a problem over and done with once a child has gone to time out and settled down. For the fast-track method, the child must continue with the potty lessons even if he is upset. If your child doesn't mind very well or you feel overwhelmed when she doesn't do what you say, this method is not for you.

So be careful! Unless you know that you have good emotional control, you may become overwhelmed to the point that you feel the urge to lash out, yell, or even become abusive. The resulting psychological trauma can be serious, setting back overall emotional development as well as potty training. Chronic problems with soiling and wetting may be the tragic result. If you do feel yourself getting upset, end the lessons immediately. Hurting your child's feelings now will definitely not help her learn to use the potty in the future!

Collect Yourself First

You're probably wondering how this method works. The answer is that children are continuously rewarded when they cooperate, but this program is very strict! Being strict is different from getting angry and punishing, however. Try to decide in advance whether you will have the patience to remain calm yet firm if your youngster doesn't cooperate.

You may have to steer your youngster to the potty and apply gentle pressure to get him to sit down if he won't voluntarily go to the potty and sit on it when told. Even if you are guiding a balky youngster back to the potty and sitting him down for the tenth time in two minutes, you must not lose patience or use more force than absolutely necessary. Even if you are very frustrated, you must give continuous neutral feedback to describe what is happening. You must praise your child despite his resistance. For instance, say:

"Good boy! You are going to the bathroom," even though you are steering him there because he won't go on his own. Say, *"Yes! You are sitting on the potty, that's good!"* as you apply light pressure to his shoulders because he resisted when you told him to sit down.

If your child does not comply with an instruction, assume he simply didn't understand you, even if you think he is being stubborn. Praise him for what he does correctly, even though he is not cooperating.

Mindful Mommy

Be strict, but be kind! It's important to remember that when a parent punishes a child for potty accidents and refusals, this can cause psychological trauma. Chronic problems with soiling and wetting may be the tragic result.

Also, remember that this is a learning process for your toddler. She may not understand everything that is expected of her. Only give one instruction at a time. Never issue a second instruction until your child completes the first. Provide lots of praise, hugs, pats, and smiles when he is learning something new or doing something difficult. However, praise becomes meaningless, even offensive, when given for something that posed no challenge. So, drop back to a smile or nod when your child complies readily or is doing something easy. However, continue to praise your child for having dry pants. Keeping them dry may remain a challenge for him for quite some time.

Is Your Tot Ready?

Because this method is truly only for older and more mature toddlers, let's consider the signs that indicate readiness. For this method to work, your toddler must already stay dry for several hours at a time, walk unassisted, and have enough motor coordination to raise and lower her pants. She must be able to imitate simple movements and learn by watching. She must be willing and able to comply with the following simple commands:

- Come when called.
- Pick up a toy when told to do so.
- Bring a familiar object such as a doll, book, or article of clothing when instructed.

- Walk to a bedroom or other room of the house when instructed.
- Place one object inside of another when directed.
- Remain seated when requested to do so.

Toddlers are never completely reliable about doing as they are told, and even typically cooperative youngsters can suddenly refuse to mind during potty training. Either your child must have a basic desire to please you or you must be exceptionally patient.

Preparing for the Day

Do your research! It's important to know what you are getting into. Before the big day, gather everything you will need. The last thing you want is to derail training by running out of the materials necessary for this method to work. You will need the following supplies:

- A doll that wets, doll bottle, and doll underpants. Children will learn the procedures for using the potty and practice them with the doll.
- Your child's favorite beverages in a variety of flavors. To ensure that youngsters get to use the potty often in a short period, they need to drink large quantities of liquids. Stock up on a variety of your child's favorite beverages.

When she tires of one flavor, you can encourage her to drink another one.

- Several kinds of salty snacks, such as chips, crackers, pretzels, and peanuts. Salt increases thirst, so stock up on several of your child's favorite salty foods. Don't rely on salted vegetable sticks, which are too filling.
- Underpants. Cloth underpants will help you and your child know when she is wet. The underpants should be several sizes too large so the child can pull them down quickly.
- A potty chair. It is helpful, though not essential, to use a chair that signals when urination begins.

Okay, here you go! Begin on a day when your child is healthy and well rested. Encourage him to drink a lot at breakfast. Try to keep him drinking at least one cup per hour throughout training so he will urinate about once every fifteen minutes. Provide salty snacks to increase thirst. Snacks and drinks double as rewards, so reward often! Arrange for brothers and sisters to be gone for the day. Turn the TV and radio off, and keep the answering machine on throughout training. Eliminate all distractions.

Using Dolls

Use the doll as an example for your child. First, put on the doll's underwear, feed it a bottle of water, and then explain that the doll has to urinate. Give your child the following instructions.

1. "Take the doll to the potty."
2. "Take off her pants."
3. "Sit her on the potty."
4. "Look between her legs."

Make the doll release water, and point out what is happening by exclaiming, "Look! The doll is urinating in the potty!" Tell your child to praise it and reward it with a pretend snack or sip of juice so he understands that using the potty is a good thing. He will be similarly praised and rewarded when he uses the potty.

Next, help your child remove the potty bowl, empty it into the toilet, flush, and return the bowl to the potty. Provide lots of verbal feedback to familiarize him with the words and phrases. Provide lots of encouragement and manual guidance to keep him moving in the right direction. Continuously describe what is happening:

"You're carrying dolly's urine to the toilet. You're putting dolly's urine in the toilet. You're flushing the toilet."

Mommy Must

While most training methods emphasize using the potty, the fast-track method emphasizes keeping pants clean and dry. In order to teach your child to recognize the feeling of wet or dry pants, show him how to feel the crotch. You can have him feel a wet paper towel and a dry one to help him get the idea.

You'll expect him to do these things after he uses the potty, too.

After the doll has wet, put dry pants on her. Have your child check the doll's pants and praise her for being dry. Then have him check his own pants. If they are dry, give him a sip of a drink he likes as a reward. If they are wet but he says, "Dry!" say, "No, they're wet." If he says, "Wet!" say, "That's right, they're wet" and change him. Tell him you will teach him to use the potty like the doll.

Spill water on the doll's pants when your child isn't looking. Have him check its pants again and tell the doll, "No, big boys and girls don't wet their pants." Do not let him punish the doll. Tell him that it needs to practice using the potty.

Have your child teach the doll to use the potty by hurrying the doll back and forth five times from where it had the "accident" to the potty, placing the doll on the potty briefly each time. In this way, your child begins learning what he must do when he has an accident. He must practice hurrying from where he had the accident to the potty so he can learn to avoid accidents.

Mommy Knows Best

After each accident, your child should practice running to the potty five times in a row. She should hurry to the potty, remove her pants, sit down for two seconds, pull her pants up, and hurry back to where she had the accident. Be forewarned: She probably won't like practicing, and might get upset.

Positive Reinforcement

Toddlers respond well to self-affirmations, much like many adults. This type of positive reinforcement is designed to help your child to create a positive mind-set. The feedback will help your child see the advantages of using the potty and help him state, to himself or aloud, his intention to be successful. Teach your child by saying:

"Daddy will be glad when you use the potty. Will you use the potty?"

Encourage your child to say "yes" or nod. Then say:

"Big boys don't wet their pants. Are you going to wet your pants?"

Encourage your child to answer "no" or shake his head. Even if he does not respond aloud, he will hopefully think the answers. You must repeat the same statements and questions often before your child will begin repeating them to himself. It's hard to predict exactly which statement will strike a chord with a particular child, so vary them. Try some of these:

"Uncle Mark goes to the potty by himself. Will you go to the potty by yourself like Uncle Mark?"

"Big boys wear underpants, not diapers. Are you a big boy?"

"Will Mama give you some chips when you urinate in the potty?"

"Daddy doesn't wet his pants. Will you wet your pants?"

"Mama doesn't like wet diapers. Will you keep your pants dry?"

"Are you going to wet your pants?"

If your child says "yes" to the last statement, answer:

"No, you are a big boy. You're going to use the potty like Daddy," or something along those lines.

Practice Makes Perfect

So, now your little one has seen the dolly use the potty. He understands that it must practice running to the potty when it has an accident. Now, it's time for your child to try using the potty herself! At this point in the training, you will use some of the lessons from the potty practice method. During potty practice, your child learns to walk to the potty chair, lower his pants, sit down, relax for up to ten minutes, get up, and pull his pants up. He will repeat the cycles of spending ten minutes on the potty and ten minutes on break until he uses the potty for the first time. Thereafter, he will spend five minutes on the potty and ten minutes on break. The first time he urinates in the potty is likely to be because he has been drinking a lot of liquids and happens to be sitting on the potty at the right time. He may not realize what happened, so watch carefully and praise him when he uses it.

After about ten minutes of trying to keep your child seated and relaxed, give him a break. If he did not urinate, watch him carefully. If you think he may need the potty, tell him to go to it quickly.

Repeat the cycle of having your child sit on the potty and take breaks until he urinates in the potty for the first time. Give him a sip and a salty snack as a reward. Show him how to wipe, raise his pants, empty the potty bowl, flush, rinse the potty bowl, replace it on the potty chair, and wash his hands. Then send him for a ten-minute break. Now you know he can relax on the potty enough to be able to use it. Thereafter, he only needs to sit on the potty for five minutes at most and then take a ten-minute break.

Learning to Relax

Although you may be anxious for your child to urinate in the potty, telling him to "try" probably won't help because he will tense up. Instead, teach

Mommy Knows Best

If you're lucky, you have a potty bowl with moisture sensors that play a tune so you can tell when your child urinates. Otherwise, have her spread her legs a bit, sit on the floor, and watch carefully. Point out when she urinates, praise her, and give her a reward.

him to relax while he is sitting. Although the goal is for him to sit for ten minutes until he uses the potty for the first time and to remain seated for five minutes at a time thereafter, many little ones would have to be forced to remain seated for longer than a minute or two. Struggles don't promote relaxation! Encourage him when he briefly sits by saying, "Good! You're sitting still." For little wrigglers, periods of decreased movement may be rare and short, so observe carefully and comment fast!

Breaks

Even though you are concentrating on getting your little one to use the potty, regular breaks to play, eat, and bathe are important. This is when your child learns to drop what he is doing and go to the potty when told. Anytime he appears to need to use the potty while on break, send him immediately. Be enthusiastic. Say,

"It looks like you need the potty! Great! Go quickly! Hurry!"

But do not argue with him. If he has an accident but has not yet managed to urinate in the potty, say:

"Don't worry. I'm going to teach you to use the potty."

And change his wet clothing. If he is on break and goes to the potty without being told, praise him heartily! He understands what he's supposed to do, and he did it! After he has used the potty once, start dealing with accidents directly.

If your child has an accident while on break, change him and wait a few minutes before telling him to sit on the potty again. There is no point in having him sit on the potty when he doesn't need to use it. Do not make him sit on the potty as punishment!

Potty Practice Prompts

Are you eying your child, just waiting for him to get that look, or squirm a bit, so you can get him to the potty before an accident happens? While you may want to avoid an accident, remember the goal is to teach him to walk to the potty without being prompted. To do this, start the first two or three potty practice sessions by saying, "Go to the potty." If your child so much as looks in the right direction, say, "That's right. Go to the potty." If he refuses, gently grasp his shoulders and steer him to the potty. Remove his pants, sit him down briefly, stand him up, and put his pants back on while saying:

Mindful Mommy

If your child is upset and frustrated, you can comfort her by reassuring her that going to the potty will get easier and she will have fewer accidents after she learns to hurry to the potty and get her pants down fast. Practice really does make perfect!

"Yes, you're practicing going to the potty. I'm taking off your pants. You're sitting down. I'm putting your pants back on. Very good! You went to the potty!"

Do not insist that an upset child remain seated on the potty for more than a few seconds. If she has a tantrum, wait until it's over before continuing potty practices. Forge ahead as soon as your child calms down. Don't let the possibility of another tantrum deter you. After a second tantrum, she will probably be more cooperative. Parents often notice a dramatic improvement after two tumultuous practice sessions. Almost every child cooperates after a third tantrum.

If at any point during a potty practice period your child walks to the potty and sits down without being prompted, express your delight in this big accomplishment!

Reducing Prompts

You can gauge how your child feels about the potty practices by the way he reacts to your prompt. Adjust your style of teaching as you go along. For example, after your child complies readily when told to go to the potty during one practice session, switch to a gentler prompt for the next one. Ask:

"Do you want to go potty?"

instead of instructing your child to go. Use the firmer "Go to the potty" statement if your child does not comply when you ask him if he needs to go.

Once your child responds to the general prompt, "Do you want to go to the potty?" by going, tell her to show you where she urinates. If she points to the potty, you can safely assume she understands its purpose. If she has also urinated in the potty at least one time, potty practice ends. If she does not point to the potty, hold more five-minute potty practice sessions alternating with ten-minute breaks until she goes to the potty when told and indicates that she understands that she is to urinate there.

No One's Perfect

Even if your child uses the potty the first time she sits on it, sooner or later an accident is bound to occur. Don't be discouraged. Most youngsters think that once training is over, they can go back to wetting in their clothes. They do not understand that they are supposed to keep using the potty, or they misjudge how long it takes to get to the potty and get their pants down. Maybe they just don't feel like using it. After your child has urinated in the potty one time and understands what she's supposed to do, respond to

Mommy Knows Best

Show your child how to grasp the front of the waistband of his pants with both hands and bend his knees so he doesn't have to lean over so far while raising and lowering his pants.

accidents by saying that they are unacceptable. Some youngsters are highly sensitive, so a little disapproval goes a long way. Be firm when you say:

"No! Don't wet your pants!" but do not yell.

Keep reminding your child to check her pants for wetness or dryness. Have her check her pants and tell you often if they are wet or dry. If they are wet, have her practice hurrying to the potty from the spot where you discovered the accident five times. Just like the dolly, each time she gets to the potty, she lowers her pants, sits briefly, raises her pants, and returns to the "scene" of the accident. Even if you feel you are nagging, keep urging her to move quickly. The secret to avoiding accidents is to hurry to the potty as soon as the urge hits, quickly removing pants, and sitting down immediately.

If your child has a tantrum when forced to practice hurrying to the potty, let the tantrum run its course before you continue. Pick up where she left off as soon as she calms down. When the practice session ends, encourage your child to participate in cleaning up and changing, but do not insist that she help.

Mommy Knows Best

Unfortunately, the fast-track method does not eliminate bedwetting. It is only for teaching children to use the potty during the day. Never chastise your child for having accidents while sleeping. Youngsters have no control over accidents in the night.

While changing your child after an accident, work on self-affirmations by saying, "Mommy doesn't like wet pants. She wants you to urinate in the potty. Will you urinate in the potty?" The goal is for your child to say or think, "I will urinate in the potty."

Slow Learners

If your child is getting tired and cranky, the lessons will be much less effective. Therefore, it's important to stop the lessons if exhaustion sets in. She can't learn if she's tired, she will just get upset and you will risk her losing interest in the future. Don't push her too hard! Continue to check your child's pants every fifteen minutes for the rest of the day. Express pleasure and give a reward of a drink when she is dry, or change her if she is wet or soiled. Otherwise, take the pressure off:

- Don't tell her to go to the potty. Just take her if it looks like she needs to use it.
- Don't have her practice running to the potty after accidents. Just change her.

Mommy Must

During potty training, you are teaching your child more than just how to use a toilet. You are teaching her about cause and effect, and about consequences. With this in mind, always have your child help clean up accidents. Give her a sponge to clean up. Tell her to remove her wet clothes and put them in the laundry area. Have her wash herself and change into clean clothes.

- Describe everything she does that is right.
- Keep her in underwear or training pants, but put on a diaper cover if she is still having accidents.

If you stop the sessions for a nap or at bedtime, pick up where you left off when she awakens. For the next two days, check your child's pants (instead of having her check them) immediately after she awakens in the morning, before and after naps, before snacks, before lunch and dinner, and before bedtime.

Consider This

Just as if your child is tired, if she is not feeling well she will not be a good student. Learning will be difficult. If she has diarrhea, a bladder infection, or an illness that prevents her from getting to the potty on time or at all, do not express displeasure or have her practice hurrying to the potty. Pick another day!

During and after training, put children over thirty months of age to bed in underwear and a waterproof diaper cover, and protect the bed with a waterproof

Mommy Must
The first day of the fast-track method, offer your little one a beverage as a reward. After the first day of training, do not offer rewards that increase urination. Try stickers or candy instead.

sheet. That way, they can easily remove their clothes if they feel well enough to go to the potty or if they awaken at night and need to use it. Put younger children to bed in diapers. They will continue to need adult help going to the potty anyway.

Success

Children are trained when they go to the potty one time without prompting and can complete all the tasks without help. After accompanying your child to the bathroom a few times to offer praise and a drink or salty snack as rewards, confine yourself to an appreciative smile when she uses the potty. If you are rigorous about enforcing practice sessions after accidents and help your child with self-affirmations, accidents usually decrease quickly. When your youngster goes two days without an accident, hold a big celebration! Help her relay the good news to other family members and friends. Bring out the cake and ice cream, and post a Potty Training Certificate on the refrigerator. While you're at it, give yourself a pat on the back, too!

Chapter 7

Is There a Pressure-Free Approach? Potties-Without-Pressure Method

POWER STRUGGLES OFTEN EMERGE when an eager parent tries to train a reluctant child. The pressure-free approach can reduce potty training stress for the whole family. In fact, the pressure-free approach recommended by the American Academy of Pediatrics can be ideal for busy families training older toddlers. It's a good way to stop power struggles before they start.

How Things Have Changed

This hands-off approach to potty training allows your child to progress at her own pace with a little guidance and support from you. The potties-without-pressure method communicates a deep, abiding respect for children's bodies and honors each youngster's need to move at his own rate. If you choose to use this method, you will not introduce the potty until age two and one-half or three. You must trust that your child possesses an inborn urge to grow up. You must have faith that he is progressing even when you cannot discern signs. With this method, you confine yourself to teaching the readiness skills, letting your child watch you use the bathroom, and treating accidents with compassion, sympathy, and understanding. The most important thing is that you should never apply pressure.

As more and more parents use the potties-without-pressure method, the average age for potty training has increased dramatically. In the 1930s, parents started training infants around three months of age. In 1946, Dr. Spock suggested waiting until the baby was seven to nine months old. In the 1950s, 90 percent of children were potty trained by age two.

In the early 1960s, author and pediatrician T. Berry Brazelton told parents to wait until their child was twenty-four to thirty months old before they started potty training. A study reported in the December 1989 issue of the *Journal of Family Practices* indicated that almost half of parents did not start potty training until after their child's second birthday. In 1999, Brazelton increased the age still further. His

Mindful Mommy

Potty training will teach you a lot about your little one's personality. As you learn more and more about your child, whether she responds well to change or whether she likes things to stay the same, cherish this time! And remember, it is now common for four-year-olds to still be in diapers.

recommendations were officially adopted by the American Academy of Pediatrics. ("Toilet Training Methods, Clinical Interventions, and Recommendations" by T. Berry Brazelton, Ann C. Stadtler, and Peter A. Gorski in *Pediatrics*, June 1999, volume 103, issue 6, p. 1359). Now, one-third of tots are still in diapers after their third birthday.

In just two generations, the knowledge that it is even possible to potty train younger children has been all but lost. Jan Faull, author of *Mommy I Have to Go Potty: A Parent's Guide to Toilet Training*, says, "pee and poop simply come out when the bladder is full" for younger children. She goes on to say: "How Grandma claims her children were completely trained at eighteen months or sooner is a mystery today."

Pros and Cons of Fooling with Tradition

The potty-without-pressure method has become very popular the last three decades. This method is great for a child who has had a negative potty experience and needs time to recover. Working parents appreciate it, especially if they cannot provide the consistency and devote the time younger toddlers require in order to learn quickly. Some children do learn in short order. But because children make all of the decisions, many progress at a snail's pace, Since so many parents are now using this method, the stigma attached to wearing diapers in preschool has all but disappeared. Increasing numbers of children are still wearing them in kindergarten.

What It Means to You

As with any potty training approach, you have to weigh the good and bad features of the method. The downside of this potty-without-pressure method is you may have to continue to be involved with diapers and cope with accidents for a long time. Moreover, even this gentle approach can lead to struggles. Some children change their mind about the potty and stop using it, but refuse to go back to diapers. If children do not wear diapers, the lack of hygiene can be a real problem in the short-term, and the smell can endure in carpeting and furniture. If they do go back to diapers, then rashes from urine and allergies from disposable diapers can lead to a whole different set of problems.

Even though this is a no-pressure approach, the recommended way to handle accidents actually does put some pressure on children.

Even the child who enjoys dumping milk and splashing in the puddles would soon get the idea that it's not good to do that. Still, such gentle handling is less destructive than yelling, punishing, and shaming.

Mindful Mommy

Confidence is a key benefit! An advantage to the potties-without-pressure method is that mastering the potty with so little help can boost children's confidence—and their parents' confidence in them.

Now let's consider some other drawbacks of this method. Think about the ongoing expense of diapers, which is tremendous. Also, the idea of children "wearing their waste" is appalling to parents that potty train infants and babies, as well as to members of the older generation. Continuing in diapers so long may be cruel if a child has chronic problems with diaper rash. Allergies to the chemicals used to manufacture disposable diapers and to sanitize cloth ones can be serious. Then there is the destructive environmental impact. Disposable diapers are the third biggest contributor to landfills. There are pros and cons for every method! You just need to weigh the two and consider whether this method is right for you, your family, and most importantly, your child!

Commitment and Self-Discipline Yours

It is impossible to see a goal through and achieve success without a couple of bumps in the road. This is especially true for young toddlers who are learning to experience the world around them for the first time, everyday! Although the lack of structure and direction of this method are fine for independent, self-motivated, self-disciplined youngsters, other toddlers will need more concrete help, limits, and structure to keep progressing. In many ways, potty training is like learning to read. Some students learn with little help and only an occasional nudge from a teacher. Those who have trouble, or little or no interest in learning, need an active, involved adult.

Patience to teach and encourage them is necessary if you use this approach. Again, some children learn virtually overnight, but many require a long time.

Consider that pet owners can housebreak a puppy in short order by taking it outside shortly after a meal and using positive reinforcement to praise it for relieving itself outdoors. However, trying to train an older animal that has developed the habit of going in the house over a period of years makes housebreaking difficult indeed. After two years of wetting and soiling, diapers can be a hard habit to break.

Still, the theory behind this extremely gentle approach is sound, and parents are wise to consider it.

It's a Waiting Game

Every toddler is different. Before you start to train your little one, with any method, you must consider his maturity level and personality! With the potty-without-pressure method, you allow your older toddler to basically teach himself. There are no reliable statistics on how quickly older toddlers complete potty training when all decisions are left to them. Once they decide to tackle it, some children master it in a day or two. Many parents report that it took one to two months; most professionals say to expect about six months. One to two years is not unheard of, either. In the past couple of decades, sales of disposable diapers in extra large and jumbo sizes have ballooned as this method has become the norm.

How will your child do with this method? Research studies show that lots of prior exposure to peers', siblings', and parents' toileting promotes learning. Common sense suggests some other factors are influential, too.

Readiness—Of all the readiness skills, being able to sense urination and bowel movements in advance and get pants on and off quickly are paramount.

Motivation—The child sees a big benefit to using the potty and wants to learn.

Help seeking—The child asks for help and is willing to follow suggestions.

Accident management—The parent remains calm and reassures the child that their accidents are nothing to be upset about.

Desire to grow up—Children want to be a "big kid" and enjoy doing things without help.

The usual pattern is for toddlers to complete bowel training before bladder training, though many finish both at the same time. However, complications due to pain from constipation or special fears about flushing tend to delay bowel training for an average of six months after bladder training is finished. Do not let your child become constipated or see his bowel movements be flushed away. Unlike other methods, in which children practice saying good-bye to their B.M.s, for this one parents don't let them see the toilet being flushed. It is believed that even if a child does not seem upset when he sees his stool being flushed down the toilet, he might have a delayed reaction and become fearful later.

A Rollercoaster of Delights and Dilemmas

There are some advantages to training an older toddler. At this age, your child may be less active than during his highly energetic two-year-old stage, making it easier for him to sit still and concentrate. He may also be generally less oppositional and have less dramatic mood swings, making him more cooperative. He probably urinates less frequently because his bladder is larger, so there will be fewer potty trips. He may be more able to delay the start of bowel movements, so he'll have more time to get to the potty when he needs to use it. Certainly, his more advanced language skills will make it easier for you to communicate with him.

Some three-year-olds learn to use the potty with so little help, it is as if they taught themselves overnight. Unfortunately, there are no guarantees. Although an older child can more readily understand that waste comes from his body, learning to recognize the sensations of needing to eliminate in advance and how to relax the sphincter may still take some time. Many older children are more compliant than they would have been during the difficult two-year-old stage, but some are more oppositional. They may not think it is worth the trouble to leave enjoyable activities to use the potty. Despite older toddlers' sometimes noisy protests about having to be changed, diaper changes can be a comforting ritual they do not want to give up.

Too many mentions of potties, questions about needing to use the potty, and warnings about impending accidents can make children feel that they are being pressured, which Brazelton says can trigger fears of failing, of disappointing their parents, or of making them angry. If you can use extreme tact, you can occasionally mention that you will help if your child ever wants to learn to use the potty. You can invite her to sit on it to hear a story. You may express your desire for her to learn to use it someday. You can communicate pleasure when your child does express an interest in using it. Otherwise, you should let your child's natural interest in learning determine when and how quickly she proceeds, and hold any dissatisfaction with her progress in check. If you decide to abandon this approach and insist that she use the potty instead of wetting and soiling, communicate your intentions clearly. In the meantime, the challenge is to trust the process instead of trying to hurry it along.

Mindful Mommy

If your child has had a bad experience in the bathroom or has a severe conflict about using the potty, he may block out his physical sensations and be unable to tell when he needs to use it. Strings of accidents don't mean that your child is defying you.

Introduction to the Potty

This method, like all of the others, requires that you be conscientious about teaching the readiness skills. But you should not make any concrete moves to introduce the potty until your child shows clear signs of wanting to learn. Signs include:

- Trying to use the potty
- Wanting to accompany other family members to the toilet
- Disliking wet diapers
- Persisting in removing diapers
- Being upset about diaper changes
- Going to a special place to wet and soil

If you have gone through this list and determined that, yes, your little one is ready to start, the first step is to let him help select a potty and choose underwear he likes. Explain that you are going to teach him to:

"Put your urine and B.M.s in the potty."

Mommy Knows Best

If you're lucky, your child will like her potty from the start. But it's possible that she will avoid it for a week or two—longer if she has had a bad prior experience, if your nervousness makes her leery of it, or if she has somehow concluded that the potty means trouble. Sit a stuffed animal on it to show her that it's safe.

But let him get to know the potty in his own way. Brazelton suggests that you not remove his clothes, believing that this could be a blow to his dignity or make him afraid.

Move Forward Slowly

Once your child can comfortably sit on the potty clothed, ask if she would like to try it without anything on her bottom.

- Ask permission before removing your child's diaper, and only remove it if she agrees.
- Then, if it looks as if she wants to, suggest she sit on her potty while you sit on the toilet.
- Explain that this is what mommies, daddies, and big kids do.

When you demonstrate and verbalize the process of using the toilet, you capitalize on your youngster's natural inclination to mimic you.

Easing into the Next Steps

After a week of demonstrating, take your child to the bathroom to remove a soiled diaper. Empty the contents into the toilet as your youngster watches. Explain that big people put their bowel movements in the toilet every day. Wait to flush until she has left the room.

On another day, ask permission to remove your child's diaper and put the potty nearby so she can use it if she wishes. If she agrees, ask if she would like to be reminded to use it about once an hour. If she says yes but doesn't respond when you remind her, that simply means she isn't ready, according to Brazelton. Drop the matter until she is. If she does use it, express mild pleasure but do not gush with delight. That takes the victory from the child. She might think she should keep using the potty to make you happy, which creates pressure.

Saying Bye-Bye to Diapers

You can lengthen the time your child spends without a diaper when you sense she might be really ready to use the potty. When an accident happens, tell her that it's okay. Remind her that someday she will be ready to use the potty like you, her older siblings, her relatives, and her friends. Until then, however, put her back in diapers.

If she refuses to wear a diaper but won't use the potty either, assume she is embroiled in an internal battle. She doesn't want to go back to wetting and soiling herself, perhaps due to pressure from peers,

Mommy Must

Although it is a habit for adults to flush immediately after they use the toilet, make sure that your child does not see you flush away his bowel movement. Even if a youngster seems unaffected at the time, the question about where that special part of him has gone can create anxieties and fears that can translate into constipation and potty refusals.

but isn't ready to move forward and use the potty, either. Only she can resolve this dilemma. Do not try to push her one way or the other.

Many children begin withholding stool as they struggle with the dilemma of not wanting to wear diapers like a baby but not being ready to join the world of big people and potties. If constipation becomes so severe that your child is in pain, it's time for you to step in and make the decision your youngster cannot bring himself to make. Put him in diapers so he can get comfortable having bowel movements again.

Disinterested Trainees

It's hard to figure out what's going on in the head of a little toddler! Some children happily use the potty for a time, and then suddenly lose interest. They would rather go back to diapers than worry about accidents and using the potty. Other times, children do not want to stop playing to use the potty and are unconcerned about accidents. If you feel angry because your youngster won't go to the potty when she needs to, consider what "won't" really means.

Mommy Knows Best

If your child wants to wear underpants but will not use the potty, she wants to grow up but isn't ready yet. The potty is a big step toward independence. Express confidence that your child will solve this hard problem in time.

When a little one is holding herself and ignores suggestions that she go to the potty, ask yourself the following questions to figure out why:

- Is it because she doesn't want to leave the fun and games?
- Is she too immersed in what she is doing to think about what is happening to her physically, even though it is obvious to you?
- Does she think she can wait a while without losing control?
- Is she afraid of growing up and needs to be a baby a while longer?

In truth, there is no way to know. If you are angry with her for having accidents, you may add to her emotional conflicts, which can slow down training even more.

Nighttime Troubles

When it comes to potty training, there is a big difference between night and day! Even if your little one uses the potty without fail during the day, she may still wet the bed. She may not awaken, or, if she does, may not feel like getting up. Carrying her to the potty at night is yet another form of pressure, according to Brazelton. Instead, when she stays dry four to six hours at a stretch during the day, try putting her to bed without a diaper to see if she is ready. If she's not, peer pressure may eventually work its wonders. When friends brag that they sleep in big-girl underwear, your child may be more motivated to try.

Many children cannot awaken until they mature sufficiently, but you can try placing the potty near your child's bed. This can help motivate your little one to use it, since he does not have to get up and walk through the dark to the bathroom by himself. You might offer to awaken him so he can use the potty before you go to bed. However, if you cannot wake him up, do not carry him there. Even if he uses it, he cannot claim the success as his own, Brazelton believes. Instead of pressuring him, suggest he wear a diaper until he is ready to use the potty at night.

What Others Think

Such a tentative attitude toward potty training may confuse your child. There is nothing to suggest that simply removing your child's diaper and teaching him to use the potty will create emotional conflicts as Brazelton suggests. Although the goal is to protect your child from any sort of pressure, this is almost

Mindful Mommy

Patience is the main training tool when it comes to potty training. It is especially needed for this method!

impossible to pull off. These days, children are social at very young ages. They attend day care or even school, play dates, and take lessons. You can't keep your youngster at home until she is fully trained!

Older people and parents in most other countries are horrified to think of waiting so long to start potty training. One of the hardest things for parents to tolerate is criticism, and you must know that waiting until your child is three and proceeding so very slowly is apt to raise a few eyebrows. Brazelton recommends letting peers apply the pressure, but peers can be very cruel.

If you use this method and your child is progressing slowly, what can you say when a friend or relative suggests that something must be terribly wrong for your preschooler not to be potty trained? Sometimes, a humorous response can relieve tensions.

- "Well, Dad, you might say that she's a little stinker in more ways than one!"
- "The experts say to wait until children give the signal. If he doesn't give it before he's eighteen, I'm going to get firm no matter what the doctors say."

Mindful Mommy

Potty training young toddlers requires more consistent involvement than many working parents can provide. If you tried other methods without success, the potty-without-pressure method might be right for your family.

- "I thought you'd never offer! I'd be glad to let her spend days with you until you've trained her. I'll take her back when you're done."

Otherwise, honesty is the way to go. Consider these options:

- "Many modern experts recommend waiting to potty train until age three, and I think they're right."
- "Between the weekend visits with her father and having to share me with the new baby, she's got enough to deal with. I don't want to add more stress to her life right now."
- "He's such a high-strung child, I've decided to wait so he'll have age and maturity on his side."
- "She's in day care during the week, so I have to use a method that doesn't require a lot of parental and caregiver involvement. Potty training takes a lot longer when there's less consistency."
- "Studies show it doesn't actually much matter when potty training starts. Children continue to have accidents until about age three anyway. There's not much point to hurrying."

As with many other aspects of parenting, potty training is a topic that always draws suggestions, opinions, and sometimes outright criticism from others. If you begin to doubt your decisions and methods, talk to your pediatrician and discuss your situation with friends and relatives.

Chapter 8

What about Accidents?

IT'S EASY TO GET frustrated and even frantic when your child has a string of accidents. Fortunately, there are lots of solutions. Many tactics are available to help little worrywarts overcome potty fears and to convince independent tots to go to the potty instead of trying to hold it. The best tricks are the games that make the potty so much fun, your child won't be able to resist using it!

Can It Be, *Another* Accident?

Not again! Another accident? What am I doing wrong? These are common thoughts for a potty coach. Keep in mind that whether these mishaps are occasional or constant, accidents really are exactly that—accidents. If you think your child is just trying to upset you when her toilet terror reaches epic proportions or when she soils and wets anywhere and everywhere, then you should definitely get professional assistance to deal with such a difficult child. Otherwise, get professional assistance to stop taking your child's problems personally. As long as you think everything is about you, you won't be objective enough to figure out how to help her. When you encounter one potty disaster after another, mustering objectivity is difficult indeed. Before you schedule your first appointment with a therapist, review the following solutions to common potty training problems.

It Can Be Terrifying

The potty training experience can be very trying for young children. If they have a bad experience, the scary memories may reappear the next time they go into a bathroom. And it's pretty easy to give up on the potty when the alternative is what they have been used to their entire lives—going in their diaper!

Unfortunately, any kind of frightening potty experience can cause your child to have a training setback. That could be:

- Falling off the potty or thinking that he might
- Falling in the toilet or imagining that he could
- Having a bad dream about a potty
- Being startled by a shout or slap while on the potty
- Hearing a loud noise while thinking about the potty

When you're two years old, fantasy and reality blur all too easily, so it's easy to imagine that Jaws lives in the bowl and then believe it's true. After imagining some dire catastrophe, your child may refuse to go near the potty. If you press him, he may become so hysterical that to insist would be to traumatize him further.

Toilets in public restrooms can be a real problem. The automatic kinds flush without warning. They are noisy, the water agitates violently, and the whoosh as the water is sucked away can be as loud as a vacuum cleaner, as if to warn him that he could be sucked away, too. Carrying a portable potty that your child can use in the car may solve the problem until he's over a public restroom phobia. However, the rest of the world's toilets may still seem unpredictable and dangerous. If he decides the one at home is out to get him, you've got a real problem.

If your child's fears center on the toilet at home, see if he will use a potty chair. If he had a scare on his potty chair, try switching to a potty seat. Try dropping the word "potty" from your vocabulary. Maybe he needs to "visit Henrietta" and "sit on her lap," or see if Mrs. Tank is "hungry" or "needs a drink." Or,

Mindful Mommy

Your child may get used to the nice, clean, safe bathroom that you have prepared for him at home and he could refuse to use other toilets. Carry a portable potty in the car for a terrified tyke.

try changing its appearance. Tie a ribbon or bow tie around its neck, affix a face with masking tape to the lid, and affix stickers inside the bowl above the water line. If that does not help, stop all practice sessions for a month to give your child time to forget. Do not even mention the potty.

A Tiger in the Tank

If your child has seen Mr. Clean leap from the bowl on TV or has heard the day care rumor that tigers or dinosaurs live in toilet water, open the tank so he can see what's inside (too small for a tiger, that's for sure). Demonstrate how to flush from inside the tank by lifting the lever, so that he can watch how the water rushes in through a tiny hole (too small for a tiger, that's for sure) then stops when the tank is full. Show him where the water leaves the toilet bowl through the little pipe in back (too small for a tiger, that's for sure).

When logic does not work (though, sometimes it does), try standing your toddler on a stool next to the toilet so he is far enough away when he urinates to be out of harm's way. Girls can stand for both urine and bowel movements by putting one foot on each side

Mommy Knows Best

If your child truly believes that there is a monster in the toilet, give him a magic wand or flashlight for protection. Explain that every time he waves the wand or shines the light around the toilet, the monster will leave or die.

of the toilet seat and bending their knees slightly so they do not make a mess. However, while you keep watch for tigers, hold your child tightly so she doesn't fall in. Since neither tigers nor Mr. Clean ever show their faces to adults, you could also sit on the toilet, spread your legs, and hold your child on your lap while he uses it.

Step by Step

You can help your child conquer her potty fears one step at a time if she is brave enough to try. Have her stand outside the open bathroom door so she can observe you while you use the toilet. Show her how to take deep breaths that will help her relax. Alert her before you flush so the sound doesn't startle her. Once she can stand in the doorway without becoming upset, she can move one baby step closer the next time and watch again. She can then take another small step nearer each day until she is close enough to put her hand on yours as you flush. Let her set the pace. When she is ready to start sitting on the potty, hold her tightly.

Praise every tiny little success for being "so brave." Point out other times during the day when she is also

Mommy Must

You can help your child through scary times by just being there. Go into the bathroom with your tot. Let her know that you are in this together, and she'll become more confident in time.

being brave, and ask her how she managed to contain her fear. This will build her awareness of her bravery and help her apply the same strategies she uses to conquer other fears.

The Differences Between Boys and Girls

If your child has been enlisting the help of you or other members of your family, he might be interested in trying out some of the things he's been seeing. Children like to experiment, and it is common to try to use the bathroom like the parent or older siblings of the opposite sex. Toddlers are barely beginning to comprehend the differences between boys and girls. Since they learn by doing, they need to go through the motions. Watching and talking are not enough to satisfy their curiosity.

- Little boys may want to use toilet paper after they urinate because Mom does. Toilet paper is fun to use and doesn't hurt anything, so let them.
- Little boys may want to stand up to urinate because Dad does. Even though their aim is poor, let them stand and show them how to push their penis down so they can give it a try. Either sitting or standing is perfectly acceptable for a tyke, though sitting is far less messy.

- Some little girls want to stand up to urinate because Dad does. Lift your daughter so that she is standing up with one foot on either side of the toilet seat, keeping your hands on her waist so she doesn't fall. Encourage her to bend her knees slightly so she doesn't make a mess.
- Some children like to sit facing the tank, and it becomes a habit. There is nothing wrong with sitting backwards! Indulge your child.

End messy experiments by saying, "Mommies and little girls/boys sit. Big boys and daddies stand up to urinate and sit to have a B.M." However, until children's curiosity is satisfied, they will probably conduct their experiments in secret, which can be far messier. It is safer—and neater—to guide them.

Out on the Town

Toddlers' ideas about potty training change constantly! If their best friend brags about making a big step, your little one might suddenly be interested. Although your child is too afraid to enter a public restroom today, soon she might want to visit every restroom in every store. When that happens, don't decide she couldn't possibly need to use the toilet yet again—nervousness about using a strange toilet can increase urinary frequency. Also, excitement or fear from being in such a novel situation may have made it hard for her to relax enough to void completely.

Don't refuse to take her because she sat for three minutes in the last bathroom and never did use the toilet. If she is nervous about whether or not you will take her when she needs to go, the likelihood of an accident increases.

If you feel as though your outings are totally centered on the restrooms and your hands are tied, they probably are. Rest assured that this, too, shall pass. Be sure to take a change of clothes just in case she is so caught up in the excitement and nervousness at the prospect of using a strange toilet, she forgets to tell you when she needs to go.

Comfort Is Key

To help lessen the likelihood that your child will feel afraid of public facilities, make it a point to use them often. Have her accompany you before you begin potty training so she can start getting used to them. Let her tear off some toilet paper for you and wash her hands so she can participate. If she becomes afraid of using public facilities after you've started potty training her, carry a folding potty chair. For this to be a solution, she must have used it at home often enough to feel comfortable with it. If she

Mommy Knows Best

If your child is afraid to use strange potties, you can purchase a portable or fold-down potty seat. Folding seats designed to fit on top of a regular toilet may not alleviate your child's fears; look for a small stand-alone folding potty chair.

is so fearful about strange bathrooms that she can't relax enough to use it, try having her use the portable potty in the car.

When in the Restroom

When you're out with a curiosity seeker, allow extra time so she can check out all the toilets in town, but beware of industrial-strength models. The sudden violent swishing and noise may frighten her so much that she becomes afraid of all public restrooms. Meanwhile, if the endless dawdling in every bathroom in every store is driving you crazy, remember that there should be something rewarding in all of this stressful potty training business. As far as many toddlers are concerned, the chance to explore the fascinating world of stalls, electric hand dryers, sinks, and faucets is about as good as it gets.

Teach your child to be respectful by not peeking under the stall to see what others are up to. Although toddlers are very curious, it's never too soon to teach good manners. Always keep your youngster within sight so she doesn't wander out and get lost. Give her something to do, such as holding your purse or the door, or engage her attention through conversation.

Toddler boys may have to be taken into the women's restroom if they don't have a dad in tow, and toddler girls will have to accompany their dads if no mom is available. Don't entrust your child to a stranger.

It Can Be Fun

Before you both feel like throwing the towel in and just giving up, think about the final outcome of potty training and how accomplished you will feel at its end. It is all too easy for potty training to become a stressful, grim affair for both parent and child. By introducing a little lightness and laughter, parents can end power struggles and turn tears to smiles.

The Tickle Me Game

Some children just cannot comprehend that they should take themselves to the potty when they need to go, no matter how many times they've been told. Mommy has been directing all the diaper and potty stuff for so long, they just don't get it. Try a conversation like the following when you think your child will soon need to use the potty. Beware! All this silliness might cause a lot of giggling, which can cause an accident.

Parent: Can you say, "I'm going to go potty?"
Child: Nods.
Parent: Can you say, "Me go potty by myself!"
Child: Me!
Parent: (Teasingly) What? Are you going to the potty by yourself? Mama's gonna get you!

Give her a tickle to get her started running, and continue the chase as long as she is heading toward the potty. Prompt by saying:

"Are you going to the potty by yourself? I'm going to tickle you!"

Stand at the bathroom door and wiggle your fingers.

"If you urinate in the potty, I'm going to tickle you!" If she goes, say, "You went potty by yourself!" and tickle her. If she doesn't, tickle her anyway so she continues to love the game.

Whether she initiates the same chasing game two seconds later or you initiate it several hours later, change the ending and do not tickle her unless she uses the potty. Look disappointed and say:

"No, you don't need the potty now." Then smile and add, "But when you use the potty, watch out! I will tickle you!"

Hopefully, once your child learns the "tickle me" game, she will initiate it. To phase it out, start to chase her, but let her go by herself and call out, "If Tanya goes potty by herself, I'm going to tickle her!

Mommy Knows Best

Accidents happen! Bending, stooping, coughing, sneezing, and laughing can cause bladder accidents. The sudden rise in abdominal pressure creates higher pressure in the bladder than in the urethra. Toddlers can't control themselves. The problem will resolve itself when they are more physically mature.

Did Tanya go potty yet?" When she calls, "I went potty," or comes to get you, go to the potty to check. If she used it, tickle her. Otherwise, say, "I don't get to tickle Tanya now. Maybe she'll use the potty later."

Nighttime Games to Get Them There on Time

Can't get your tyke to use the potty at night? She will have to get out of bed if she wants to see the glowing green water, which can only be detected when the bathroom is dark and a Poti Lite is hanging in the toilet bowl. She may think this product is way cool, and be glad to leave her covers to see it! The unit sits under the toilet seat with the batteries hanging outside the bowl and a flexible arm with a light extending inside. The Poti Lite can be purchased online.

Before the Buzzer

See if your child can "beat the clock" by using the potty before the alarm sounds to signal the start of his next potty practice session or if he can "beat the clock" by using the potty before his required session ends.

The problem with trying to beat the clock is that you must never set your child up to fail. Be aware that the excitement of this race against time can cause the kind of tension that keeps youngsters from being able to relax enough to use the potty or cause them to lose control and have an accident.

Hold It!

If you see your child dancing about and holding his crotch to avoid an accident, you may bad for insisting that he go to the potty. But it's important that he heed nature's call. Besides increasing the risk of accidents, holding in urine for long periods increases the risk of bladder infection. Carried to an extreme, containing urine can stretch the bladder, damaging the muscles. That makes it harder for children to sense the contractions that signal their need to relieve themselves.

Timed Sits

Even if you don't prompt your child to hold it, she may try. If she insists on holding it to the point of discomfort or accidents, set an alarm and take her to the potty every hour. Set a timer, and have her sit for a few minutes. Once she learns she must sit out the time whether or not she urinates, and understands that you are equally pleased either way, she won't be in such a hurry and should be able to relax. When she does use the potty, do not make a big deal out of it. Just say:

"There's your urine! I bet you feel better now."

Mindful Mommy

Some children leak additional urine right after they use the potty. So a few minutes after your child uses it, ask her to check her pants. If she is damp, repeat the after-potty pants checks each time she urinates. If leakage is a regular occurrence, notify her pediatrician.

Where Do Pee and Poop Belong?

At certain ages, knowing that Mom wants her to "go" may be enough for a tot to decide she doesn't want to. The way out of this impasse is to help her understand that it is not a matter of what you want or what she wants. It's what "Pee" and "Poop" want. And what they want, of course, is to go to their home! Tell your child so.

When your child is trying to prevent urination or the start of a bowel movement, explain that Pee and Poop are trying to get her attention so she will take them where they want to be—in the potty. Or, tell her they are begging her to put them where they belong—in the potty. Or, say that they are begging to go to their home—in the potty.

If your child is caught up in a struggle with herself, and holding in waste to the point of pain, explain that Pee and Poop need her help to get "home." What she needs to do is to sit on the potty and relax. It might help her to lie down and have her tummy rubbed. Suggest that drinking more water and eating more fruit and vegetables help make Pee and Poop strong enough to get out. Although she would not

Mommy Knows Best

Times have changed. In the past, teaching children to "hold it" was thought to strengthen the sphincter muscles and help prevent wetting. Now this is believed to stretch and potentially damage them, which lessens bladder control.

make the culinary sacrifice for herself, she might be willing to do it for them.

The Circle of Life

If children are upset about having their B.M.s flushed away, teaching them about the circle of life may comfort them. Explain that her B.M. is going to feed the trees and flowers so the plants will grow tall and beautiful. The birds and other animals eat the plants so they can grow big and strong and feed their babies.

From that kind of story, one toddler instantly overcame his reluctance about having bowel movements in the potty. His parents weren't quite sure what happened until they heard their chronically constipated son happily explaining to his sister that the birds "eat my marbles." Thankfully, he was willing to do his part for the sake of the food chain.

Toddlers' Favorite Playthings

If your child becomes attached to the B.M. he created and wants to save it, this is normal! Toddlers are famous for being very possessive of their little lumps and piles. Whatever goes in the potty bowl or toilet is going to end up being flushed away, and that thought may be too terrible for a child to bear. Diapers, of course, are fine—no matter that your child has watched you scrape her gems into the toilet a million times. Who can fathom toddler logic? If your toddler is upset about having her B.M.s flushed away after she sits on the potty, the simplest solution is to close the toilet lid and wait to flush until she is out of the room.

Homemade Toys

If your child is particularly attached to her B.Ms, she may decide they aren't safe with you or anybody else. Anyway, they're hers—so what right has anyone else to take them away? She may retreat to a special place to have bowel movements and hide what she's up to, then play with her great homemade toys. No, you don't have a deranged child on your hands. You can't let her do that, though. Putting wet or dirty fingers in her mouth could make her ill. Playing with her homemade Play Dough must be a "no-no."

Getting Her into the Bathroom

It is very important to know when your child is passing waste so you can prevent her from playing in it! If she won't use the potty just yet, try to get her at least to do her business in the bathroom. The habit of standing or squatting to defecate may make sitting feel too awkward. If she uses a potty seat, provide a stool to support her feet so she can push to have a bowel movement. If she won't sit down for B.M.s, contrive a way for her to stand or squat. Provide a container that's small enough so she can stand over it but big enough so aiming isn't a problem. Or, see if she will stand or squat over paper towels.

If she must have a diaper, perhaps she can stand over it instead of wearing it. By placing a stack of clean diapers next to the potty, she can simply take one when needed. Teach her to fold soiled diapers carefully so she doesn't touch the contents. Find a mutually agreeable place to store her precious packet, such as in a lidded diaper pail. If she hides when having B.M.s, she may need privacy. Stand outside the bathroom door.

If They Refuse to Use the Bathroom

If your child won't have bowel movements in the bathroom, show him how to lay out a towel to protect carpeting. Teach him to take the dirty diaper to you afterward so you can help him clean up.

To help your child take the next step, suggest that he first put his B.M. in the potty, and promise to put it in a diaper for him afterward. (You can retrieve it with a serving ladle.) In that way, your child can become accustomed to using the potty and his B.M. still ends up in what he considers the right place.

Mindful Mommy

Constipation can be tricky. It can stop tots from having B.M.s or cause uncontrollable soiling, because softer feces leak around the hard mass. Children cannot control the leakage. Try to find out what is causing hard stool so you can soften it.

Preventing Accidents

Power struggles only slow potty training. If your child is being particularly stubborn, it does not mean that he is purposely trying to upset you. He's not consciously thinking,

"I'll show Mom that she can't make me do this! I'll mess in my pants just to upset her!"

Rather, the struggle is unconscious. Toddlers can often sense parents' emotions. Many children avoid all thoughts about the potty because it is a source of tension, parental anger, and personal defeat. When forced to sit on the potty, they don't know how to expel urine or how to relax the sphincter muscles to release stool. The minute another miserable potty session has ended and they put the whole matter out of their minds, they relax, and suddenly the urine or stool begins to flow. If they get in trouble for having another accident, they will be even tenser the next time they're taken to the potty. A vicious cycle develops, and the problem gets worse and worse.

Mommy Knows Best

Do not restrict your child's fluid intake to cut down on daytime bladder accidents! The urinary urge intensifies when urine is more concentrated. Dehydration can cause constipation, which can create even bigger potty training problems.

The most effective solution is to handle accidents as calmly as possible. Avoid reproaching your child but insist that he participate by changing his clothes and helping with cleanup. Until he is ready to comply, assign a time-out. If you are convinced he has accidents just to get you, don't get upset. He will soon lose his motivation to wet and soil.

Teaching Through Tough Love

By age three children should be able to help clean up accidents. There are compelling reasons for them to participate if they are destroying the carpet, generating tons of laundry, and making no effort to use the potty. It may be difficult not to be angry, but it is very important that you remain calm and matter of fact. Your role is to teach. If you can't get your child to use the potty, teach him to help with cleanup.

- Put a stepstool by the washer.
- Show your child how to put the dirty clothes in the washer, push the button, and lower the lid.

Supervise carefully throughout this process. Store detergent and cleaning solvents where your child can't reach them, and add them to the laundry yourself. Do not ever let your child touch these poisons! Afterward, have him help transfer the clothes to the dryer and push the button to start it. Then have him put the clean clothes in the clothesbasket. He can work on his colors and shapes and sizes while learning to make piles of diapers and match socks (great for cognitive development) while you fold and stack. Then, help him put the clothes away in drawers he can reach so he can change himself with as little help as possible.

As you will soon discover, making your child help clean up accidents is not abusive. On the contrary, he will probably have so much fun, your desire to make him suffer so he'll stop having accidents will be thwarted. Might he want to have another accident just so he can do all that great laundry stuff again? Probably. Find more laundry he can help with, but do not try to ruin his fun. Potty training will end in a month or a year—his laundry skills can make your life easier for the next two decades and serve him well for the rest of his life! Grin and bear it until the novelty wears off. When it does—and it will—perhaps he will be more motivated not to have accidents.

Less Forgetfulness

If you have tried everything you can think of and your child keeps forgetting to go to the potty, perhaps having her go about bare-bottomed can help her remember. Turn up the thermostat, tell her not to have an accident, and remind her to use the potty

Mindful Mommy

Most parenting books say never to go back to diapers after putting a youngster in underpants. But why continue to beat your head against the wall, make your youngster miserable, and ruin the carpet? If he isn't ready, he just isn't. Maybe in a month he will be!

when it looks like she might need to. Like tying a string around a finger, the unusual sensation of having nothing on her bottom may help her remember. Girls can go naked under a dress; it might work for a boy to wear pants without underwear. If an accident happens, do not admonish or punish. Just start teaching your child how to help with cleanup.

When he is holding himself or looks like he needs to use the potty, ask if he wants to go to the potty or wants you to bring it to him. Sometimes offering a choice instead of telling toddlers what to do works better. If he declines both, tell him if he has an accident, he will have to put away his toys until he helps clean up and changes his clothes. If he does have an accident, be true to your word!

If your child continues to have accidents, then it's time to teach some basic janitorial skills.

Oops—They Happen

Cheer up your little overachiever by reassuring her that eventually she will remember to listen to her body when it announces that it is time for her urine to come out. Until then, accidents will happen. They are not the end of the world! Teach her to say,

Mommy Must

Involve you toddler in every aspect of potty training. For example, teach him to clean himself up by popping him into the tub after accidents. That way, he learns to take responsibility for himself even if he's not using the potty.

"Oops!" Use the problem-solving strategies explained earlier in this book; help her understand that there is a way to fix every mistake.

Venturing Out Alone

Up until now, you have been telling your child to drop everything and call you so you can help him get to the potty and not have an accident. Do you find yourself thinking, "Again? No, he couldn't really need to use it so soon." Nevertheless, you drop what you are doing and run to help him. Of course, when you two get to the bathroom, he doesn't need to go. What can you do? Swallow your irritation. Praise his "good intentions." Be true to the lesson you've been trying so hard to teach: When nature calls, everything else must be put on hold. Yes, it's hard being a parent. I know it can be frustrating. I understand it's a pain. But just do it. Respond every single time he calls for potty help.

Talk Your Way to Success

Even though most toddlers are not very verbal, they can listen and hear what you have to say—so talk to your child. Some children even respond well to sit-down conversations. In the interest of moving potty training forward, it's certainly worth trying to have a serious talk about the problems.

Please—A Magic Word

After age three, most youngsters develop the charming characteristic of being able to consider other people's perspectives and points of view. They may pick wildflower bouquets to give as presents, make pictures for parents' refrigerators, or cheer up friends who are feeling sad. In other words, your child may be willing to do you a favor. Try saying:

"Mommy doesn't like accidents. She doesn't like doing all that laundry. Please go to the potty, OK? That would be such a nice present for me!"

Of course, most toddlers know Mommy is supposed to take care of them; they are not supposed to have to take care of Mommy. Still, give it a shot. Just don't take a negative answer personally. It's not you, it's not them; it's the age.

Mom's Method

If you are limping along with intermittent accidents because your child is too busy to be bothered going to the potty, try having what my own mother called "the conversation."

"In this house, we all use the potty. That includes you. Sonnas do not make these kinds of messes! Do you understand?" (Pause for effect.) *"Do I need to remind you or will you just go?"*

Regardless of the answer, the next time baby brother looked like he needed to go, she would say:

"Remember! In this house, we all use the potty. Sonnas do not make messes!"

All of her "Sonnas do this" and "Sonnas don't do that" lines, used on important occasions, had already instilled a sense of family pride. The conversation worked.

If it hadn't, she would have followed up with:

"I guess you do need me to remind you to use the potty, since you can't remember that Sonnas do not wet their clothes. You may wear diapers when the baby sitter is here, but when you're with me, you will use the potty like the rest of the family."

Then there would have been once-an-hour potty practices during which a little Sonna either used it right away or sat for a minute or two to "think about why Sonnas use the potty instead of making messes." She was that kind of mom.

Become a Counselor

When potty training seems hopelessly stalled, sometimes a brief counseling session can help. When your child is calm, find a private place for a quiet talk. Look your youngster in the eye and probe her negative feelings about the potty by saying, "You don't like to use the potty, do you?"

Then pause. Make it a long one. Maybe you will get a small shake of the head or nod. Maybe you will only see a tense expression, notice a quick subject change, or observe misbehavior meant to distract you. Do not be distracted. Instead, gently ask, "Honey, why don't you like to go to the potty?"

Give your child time to think about your questions, but do not expect her to answer. She probably doesn't know and couldn't tell you even if she did. Hopefully, your question will encourage her to ponder the matter. Once she can identify the problem, she will have taken the first step to solving it.

Start to wind down your little counseling session by providing reassurance:

"Going to the potty may seem hard right now, but it will get easier with time and practice."

Your words may be incomprehensible, but your reassuring tone will communicate that you are on her side.

After your words (or tone) have had time to sink in, offer anything you can think of to help her:

Mindful Mommy

Your child may not respond to you when you talk to him. Nevertheless, he may listen and think about what you say. If you think your child never listens, you are probably wrong. Even if your words do not get through, your tone does.

"Would you like to go back to diapers for a while?"
(if she has not been wearing them)

"Would it help if I told you when to go to the potty?"
(if you have been letting her decide on her own)

"Would it help if I gave you a surprise every time you used the potty?" *(if she is not already receiving rewards)*

Again, do not expect a response. If you do get one, treat her comments with deep respect. If you do not come up with any workable solutions or new things to try, conclude with,

"If Mommy can help you with the potty, let me know."

And give her a reassuring hug and a kiss. If nothing else, this gesture should help to defuse power struggles.

Do not be surprised if a day or a week later your child suddenly reveals something that helps to explain at least part of the problem. She may say you should put diapers on her instead of on her little brother, which may mean she wishes she could be the baby again instead of a big girl who has to cope with potties. She may suddenly get upset because she wants her B.M. back after it has been flushed away, letting you know that it bothers her when it disappears down the drain. She may suddenly dissolve into tears when you suggest she put aside her toys to use the bathroom, letting you know how she longs for the more carefree days when she didn't have to worry about accidents all the time.

Comfort your child, sympathize with her plight, and reassure her that she is still your baby. Continue your usual potty routines and requirements and try to reduce other pressures. Try not to push her to grow up too fast. To the extent that it's possible, let her be what she is: a baby in oh-so-many ways.

Chapter 9

How Can We Keep My Little One Healthy?

IT IS EASY TO get caught up in challenge of potty training and to lose sight of the big picture: health and hygiene. It's important to consider the long-term goal, even if you are consumed with trying to tackle the day-to-day challenges. Some of the things to keep in mind are cleanliness, a healthy diet, and lots of exercise. The habits your child develops during potty training may last for years—perhaps for a lifetime.

Teaching Hygiene

Toddlers are very impressionable. They are experiencing the world for the first time and learning new things everyday. The habits children develop when learning to use the potty are likely to last a lifetime. It is important to teach them to wash their hands and wipe properly, and to rinse the potty bowl and flush the toilet after each use.

Potty training time is a good time to teach other points of etiquette, too, such as putting down the toilet seat and lid, wiping up splashes in the sink after hand washing, and straightening the towel before dashing off to play. Toddler boys need to be taught to pay attention when they urinate so they do not spray the floor and walls, and to clean up if they do.

- Teach your youngster to do his part to help maintain a room of the house he will use lots in the years to come.

Parents spend so much time dealing with their youngsters' waste, they can begin to take it for granted to the point that they forget to follow basic rules of hygiene. After spending so much time struggling with potty training problems and accidents, you may not want to make an issue of wiping and hand washing. Good hygiene really is important for your entire family's health. Be sure to give it the attention it deserves.

Wait—Wash Those Hands

Hand washing is an important habit to instill. It does more than keep toddlers' hands pretty and presentable; it protects children from disease. Failure to wash hands properly after using the toilet can cause illness—and it often does! Toddlers will inevitably get stool on their hands when they wipe themselves, as will caregivers when they change diapers and handle soiled laundry. Even traces too small to be seen contain germs. If a contaminated hand has a small cut, or if it touches the mouth or an eye, germs that cause illness enter the body. Be very careful about washing your hands after you touch soiled diapers and laundry. Have your child come to you for a clean hands check after he has used the potty by himself.

It is sometimes hard to stay just as germ-free in public as at home. In fact, public restrooms are especially germ-filled. Studies show that about a third of people do not wash their hands at all, and another third don't do it correctly. Consequently, almost every surface is contaminated. Here are instructions on how to get the hand-washing job done right:

- Wet hands.
- Use liquid soap whenever possible; avoid wet bar soap.
- Rub hands vigorously to dislodge microscopic bacteria and viruses from ALL areas of the skin for fifteen to twenty-five seconds.
- Rinse thoroughly.
- Dry hands on a clean, dry towel.

There are hundreds of antibacterial soaps on the store shelves today, but think before you use these too often. Some scientists warn that the widespread use of antibacterial soaps will result in resistant superbugs, as has happened from antibiotics and insecticides. As long as you wash your hands well, you and your child can stick to plain soap and still be clean!

Wiping Dos and Don'ts

Even if your little one is fully potty trained, you will probably need to help her out with wiping herself for a couple of years. Most children will not do a very good job of wiping themselves until kindergarten. Besides their lack of practice, their arms are just too short for their bodies, so they have a hard time reaching their bottoms. Teach your child to use several small pieces of toilet paper to clean himself, tossing each one as it becomes soiled. This is far more effective than toddlers' natural tendency to use a single big wad. Moistened towelettes can do an even better job. Children will need adult help to use them at first, too.

Starting at the vagina, girls should wipe forward with clean tissue after urinating so as not to get bacteria in the vagina or urethra. For the same reason, they should start just behind the vagina and wipe back along their buttocks after a bowel movement.

Keeping the Penis Clean

You need to make a special effort to keep the penis of an uncircumcised boy clean in order to reduce the risk of infection. The foreskin of an uncircumcised infant cannot be pulled back, but make it a habit to lift the foreskin gently as soon as it begins to loosen, and wash the area carefully during each bath to prevent infection. Do this by gently wiping with a soft washcloth that has been moistened with warm water. Teach your tot how to do the same when he is old enough. When the foreskin is fully retractable, it can be folded back over the penis like the cuff of a shirt sleeve over an arm. Be sure your child returns it to its normal position after urinating or washing himself. If the foreskin is left folded, it can act like a rubber band. The constriction can cause problems that are serious enough to require medical treatment.

Diaper Rash, but Not for Much Longer

Potty training is the best cure for diaper rash! While your little one is still in diapers, there are things you can do to help alleviate the irritation. Diaper rash is usually caused by urine residue on skin. Because urine is very acidic, it can wreak havoc with delicate baby skin. To help clear up diaper rash, change wet diapers frequently. Allergies can make skin problems worse, so try switching brands of disposables or use cloth diapers. Avoid wipes that contain alcohol, which is drying. Gently blot the skin instead of rubbing it.

Protect against chafing by applying a cream containing zinc oxide. If there is irritation on the sides of the groin or around the waist, fold disposable diapers

Mommy Knows Best

While we have store-bought baby powders today, back in the late 1800s to mid 1900s, parents dusted babies with plain white flour to keep them dry. To keep flour from turning into dough when wet, bake it at 300 degrees, stirring occasionally until it is uniformly brown!

so the plastic liners face out and don't touch the skin. Letting your child go bare-bottomed for ten minutes to be sure he is completely dry before putting on a clean diaper can help eliminate diaper rash. If a rash worsens or persists for three days, it may be a yeast infection. See your pediatrician for a prescription to treat it.

Bronchial irritants, including toluene, xylene, ethylbenzene, styrene, and isopropylbenzene, are among the chemicals typically found in disposable diapers, according to a lead researcher for the diaper study summarized in a report entitled, "Acute Respiratory Effects of Diaper Emissions." The outgassing of a straight-from-the-package diaper in a medium-sized room was high enough to produce asthma-like symptoms ("Acute Respiratory Effects of Diaper Emissions," by Rosalind Anderson and Julius Anderson. *Archives of Environmental Health*, 54, October 1999). If you see crystallized gel oozing on your child's bottom, that's part of the chemical brew used to enhance disposable diapers' absorbency. Stick with cloth!

Bladder Health

It is important to give your little one lots to drink. Hydration is important for many reasons, including regular bowel movements, frequent urination, and bladder health. You can give your child juices and water or a combination of the two. Drinking lots of water promotes frequent urination, which decreases the risk of bladder infections..

Avoid Bladder Infections

Bladder infections happen throughout life, but your toddler might not know what her pain is or where it is coming from. As her mommy, you should get to know the signs! Bladder infections are more common in girls because the urethra is short. In wiping after bowel movements, girls can get a bit of stool on the urethral opening. However, boys can and do get bladder infections, too. Bladder infections can increase the frequency of urination. They may also create an urgency so intense, children can't get to the potty in time.

The typical symptom is blood in the urine, which turns it cloudy or pink. There may be a spot of blood on the toilet tissue after urination. Bladder infections can also cause loss of bladder control, frequent and/ or painful urination, pain just above the pubic area or on the side, fever, and lethargy. They can be serious, so see your doctor fast.

Mommy Must

Keep a close eye on your baby's genitals while you are changing their diapers or teaching him to use the potty. If you spot something odd, contact your doctor. Discharges from the penis are rare before puberty, but if you notice one, your child might have an infection.

Ouch—Urinary Tract Infections

Toddler logic has it that what comes out should go in, so most boys will at some point use a squeeze bottle or squirt gun in the bathtub and inject some water into their personal fountain. The result can be a urinary tract infection. Be sure to tell your child that he must never put water or anything else in his penis. Hope for the best but be prepared for the worst. Just as toddlers are driven to insert beans in their ears and peas into their nostrils, they are compelled to insert water into their penis.

Oil from the skin and small quantities of urine can easily become trapped under the foreskin if an uncircumcised penis is not cleaned properly, which can cause infection. Pus signals the presence of an infection that requires medical attention. In addition, associated swelling can prevent the flow of urine. Contact your doctor immediately.

A Lesson in Leakage

Additional leakage after urinating can signal a physical malformation correctable by surgery, so check your child's pants for moisture a minute or two after he uses the potty. Otherwise, you might think he had

Mindful Mommy

You should consult a doctor if your little one experiences frequent urination, few periods of being dry, or painful urination. These could be a sign of a bladder infection or even diabetes—so check it out.

an accident an hour later when he didn't. Also, your child's stream of urine should be strong and steady. See your doctor if it tends to trickle out or flows in erratic spurts, even when your child urinates a large quantity. Infants do this, but toddlers should not.

Bowel Health

Every child poops, but not always the same amount. Some have bowel movements daily, some many times a day, some only once every few days. It doesn't matter how often your child has bowel movements. The issue is whether the stool is too hard (constipation) or too runny (diarrhea). Some children even have a natural tendency to be constipated or easily get diarrhea. Unless your child is ill, diet is the best way to promote regularity. Eating a lot of highly processed (a.k.a. "junk") foods causes constipation, because they are absorbed into the system so completely, all that remains is a hard, heavy mass. The best treatment for constipation is a diet rich in fruits, vegetables, and whole grains (especially bran, brown rice, whole wheat, and oats) to add lightweight bulk, and lots of water to soften the stool.

Pain and Pressure of Constipation

Serious problems with constipation can complicate potty training. Small hard "marbles" don't usually cause a problem, but wide stool can be painful to pass and cause tears that take time to heal. Small drops of blood on underwear or toilet paper may signal that this has happened. Rectal itchiness occurs as the tears start to heal. Gently wash the anus with soap and water after each bowel movement, and have your youngster soak in a warm bath to ease the pain. Put a dab of petroleum jelly on your finger and insert it into your child's rectum to help soothe and protect the sore area.

The added pressure on the bladder from a lot of hard stool can give children less time to get to the potty, so they have more wetting accidents. A full bowel leaves less room for the bladder. It can't hold as much liquid, so urination is more frequent. The pain of constipation can blur the sensation of needing to urinate, so children have difficulty realizing when they need to use the potty.

Psychological Constipation

With diets rich in junk food and low in fiber, it's no wonder so many toddlers are constipated. But it's not all physical—in fact, more often than not, a child's inability to use the use the potty is due to a mental block. One painful bowel movement can

Mommy Must

To avoid constipation, give your child snacks of veggies and fruits and see that he gets plenty of exercise. To promote exercise, turn off the TV and clear an area of the house suitable for vigorous play.

make toddlers afraid to have another. Your little one's emotions can undermine his ability to relax the anal sphincter in order to release stool. The result is "psychological constipation." Some causes may be:

- Sitting on a cold toilet seat
- Potentially being splashed by cold water (if a potty seat is used)
- Watching part of oneself being discarded and sucked down a noisy drain
- Losing the special one-on-one time while a beloved parent wipes and cleans and rubs them with sweet-smelling creams and lotions

Stress during potty training can cause tension that creates psychological constipation.

Softening the stool to ensure bowel movements do not hurt can help. If shaping up your child's diet isn't enough, mineral oil will make it impossible for your youngster to hold back a bowel movement. The oil softens the stool so passing a B.M. doesn't hurt. But is dosing a youngster with mineral oil to pry out feces an invasion of bodily integrity? Consult your conscience as well as your pediatrician to decide. If you use mineral oil, inquire about the need for vitamin supplements.

Remember that it's one thing to administer laxatives, stool softeners, and enemas to youngsters who are suffering from constipation or impaction because a pediatrician prescribed them. It's quite another to dose children with laxatives instead of straightening out their diet. Using laxatives to ensure your child has bowel movements at particular times so you can get her on the potty should be considered some sort of abuse. Don't do it!

Diarrhea

Diarrhea can put a halt to potty training progress in a second! Children don't have much if any bowel control during even minor bouts of diarrhea. Don't pressure your child about accidents; he can't control himself. Avoid foods that have a laxative effect, especially raw fruits and vegetables and concentrated fruit juices. Until he's better, put him in diapers and forget potty training.

The main risk of diarrhea is dehydration, which is dangerous if it goes on for very long. It can become dangerous very quickly if there is also vomiting and high fever. Taken to an extreme, diarrhea can be fatal. Lost minerals such as chloride, sodium, and potassium must be replaced quickly. Give your child Gatorade or another electrolyte solution. Contact

Mindful Mommy

Potty training can be considered a misnomer. It is actually potty teaching! As you experience the power of positive teaching methods to help her learn quickly and easily, you will learn the most powerful lesson of all: how to be a really wonderful parent.

your doctor if you note any signs that serious trouble is brewing:

- Cracked lips
- Decreased urination
- Darker or deeper yellow color of urine
- Urine that appears to have crystals
- A sunken soft spot on the head of a young toddler
- Listlessness

Head straight for the emergency room and try to get her to drink a Gatorade type preparation en route if there are no tears when crying, her cry is weak, her breathing is shallow, the surface of her tongue is dry, her skin feels cool, the skin of her hands and feet is mottled, her eyes appear sunken, she hasn't urinated for four hours, her skin is less wrinkled and elastic, or if after pinching a finger or toe, her skin takes more than a second to return to normal color. This test assumes the child has been in a warm room.

Penis Health

As your baby becomes a toddler, his body will be growing everyday. Your newborn's foreskin is fully attached to the penis. The foreskin gradually begins to loosen, and by age one the glans at the tip of the penis itself should be visible. Most boys' foreskin is fully retractable by age four or five, although for a significant percentage of children this doesn't occur until much later. When it does, the foreskin can be folded back over the penis so that it is fully exposed for proper cleaning. The foreskin must never be left folded. That is dangerous and requires an immediate doctor's visit if the penis swells to the point that the foreskin cannot be readily unfolded. Often cold compresses and medications to reduce the swelling are sufficient to return it to normal, but minor surgery is sometimes required to relieve the constriction.

Because uncircumcised penises require special care, parents commonly opt to have the foreskin surgically removed. Although this custom is on the wane, many people still claim there are only benefits to circumcising a child. In fact, a circumcised penis is easier to clean, which reduces the risk of infection. However, infants do feel the pain from the surgery. Moreover, the widespread belief that circumcision does not impact adult sexual functioning is false. The exposed tip loses a good deal of sensitivity.

Potty Training and Food Allergies

As you challenge your toddler to try new things, food being one of them, it is important to keep an eye out for allergies! Food allergies can affect the bowel and bladder, causing diarrhea, constipation, and bladder irritation. Talk to your pediatrician about eliminating foods that may be causing problems from your child's diet. The usual procedure is to eliminate one item for ten days to two weeks to see if the problem improves, only to recur when the food is eaten once again. The following are common culprits:

- Milk and dairy products. (Remember that cheese and butter contain milk!)
- Carbonated beverages.
- Artificial colors and sweeteners.
- Citric acid and vitamin C.
- Melons, especially watermelon and cantaloupe.
- Any other foods to which your child might be allergic.

Important, Fluid Intake

Toddlers need four to six cups of fluid daily under normal circumstances—more in hot weather or if they are ill with fever, vomiting, or diarrhea. Besides water (from the tap or bottled; plain or carbonated), good sources include soup, juice, and milk. However, milk provides only $2/3$ cup of fluid per cup; the rest is solids.

Chapter 10

What If Something Is Wrong?

POTTY TRAINING ISN'T EASY! And it isn't a perfect practice. Many children can overcome some potty training hurdles but face others. Even though your little one sometimes knows what he's doing, does he continue to wet the bed at night? Have chronic wetting or soiling accidents? Have continuing problems with constipation or urination? It's important to figure out if you and your child can tackle these problems on your own or if you need some help from a pediatrician.

How and Where to Get Help

If you've been trying to potty train your child for a long time and you're having problems, the person to turn to for help is your child's pediatrician. Doctors with this specialty work with potty training problems day in and day out, and are extremely knowledge-able about the subject. In addition to their technical knowledge, pediatricians have dealt with hundreds or even thousands of youngsters, which gives them a substantial basis for comparison. Although it may be true that no one knows your child as well as you do, professionals are in a better position to be objective.

When talking to your child's doctor, be honest and forthcoming when sharing your potty training problems, as well as the steps you have taken to correct them—even if it means admitting things that you have said and done that you think were wrong.

To hold back is to do your child and yourself a disservice. The truth is that few parents feel very confident about how they have handled all of the problems that arise during potty training. And if they do, they probably shouldn't!

If you don't feel comfortable confiding in your child's pediatrician, schedule some interviews with different doctors. Since hearing other parents' struggles can give you a new perspective on your own, consider joining a parenting group, too.

Avoid Wetness at Night

Although your child is potty trained during the day, she may still wet the bed at night. There are a number of things that you can do to help ensure that your little one gets to the potty during the night. Wearing diapers to bed encourages a continuation of the habit of wetting and soiling. Sleepy children cannot use the potty easily if they are in diapers. Instead, use a rubber pad to protect the bed and put waterproof pants over pull-ups so your child can get them off to use the potty at night. Or, try putting a PODS inside his regular underwear.

Although full-blown fears of the dark do not typically develop until after age three, precocious children may feel uneasy at night at younger ages. Move the potty chair into the bedroom or light the way to the bathroom with nightlights. The prospect of company can be an incentive for a little one to get out of bed at night, so encourage your child to awaken you so you can take him to the potty.

Do not let your youngster drink a lot of liquids after dinner, and take her to the potty before she goes to bed. Take her before you go to bed, too, and set an alarm to awaken yourself so you can take her to the bathroom once or twice a night. That may help her develop the habit of waking up to use the potty once she is mature enough.

In the meantime, be patient. Most children have been conditioned to urinate in bed for several years. Disposable diapers reduce the discomfort of wetting to the point that many youngsters don't awaken even after they have had an accident. Even if they are in cloth and can feel the wetness, they may not awaken because they simply sleep too deeply.

Don't Let the Bedwetting Blues
Get You Down

There are three main causes of bedwetting: motivational, physical, and "deep sleep." It can be hard to tell whether bedwetting stems from the I-don't-feel-like-getting-out-of-bed-to-use-the-potty-at-night motivational problems as most parents tend to think at first. Most bedwetting is caused by deep sleep.

Physical Problems

There are some physical problems that affect nighttime incontinence. Physical problems ranging from small bladder size to a bladder infection can cause incontinence. Many such problems can be easily corrected. Sleep apnea can prevent children from awakening so they can use the potty; the brain never receives the bladder's signal that it is full. Eventually the sphincter gives way, causing an accident. If apnea is due to problems with the adenoids and tonsils, it can be easily treated. Apnea is sometimes difficult to diagnose. Obvious symptoms may only be present at night, so children can appear healthy when examined by a doctor during the day. Bedwetting also can infrequently be the result of bladder infection, a hormone deficiency, petit mal seizures, diabetes, a small bladder, a physical abnormality or malformation, or a central nervous system disorder. Nevertheless, such physical problems are rare. Altogether, they are believed to affect less than 3 percent of children.

Deep Sleep

The usual problem, which causes millions of youngsters to wet the bed, is deep sleep. Children sleep so soundly, they simply don't awaken so they can use the potty. They may have some dry nights, but if they can't manage to go a full month without wetting the bed, the diagnosis is likely to be "primary enuresis." What keeps them from awakening isn't understood.

Boys, who are known to mature more slowly than girls, are more likely to be bedwetters, and since 15 percent of bedwetters spontaneously outgrow the problem every year, physical maturity is thought to be a factor. Most bedwetters have relatives who had the same problem as children, so heredity is thought to play a role.

Children who stay dry every night for a month and then start wetting the bed again probably have "secondary enuresis." As many as 25 percent of children have relapses after they have been dry at night for six months or longer. (*The Gale Encyclopedia of Childhood and Adolescence*, Jerome Kagan, Executive Editor; Susan B. Gall, Managing Editor. Detroit, Mich.: Gale Research, 1998). The usual causes are fatigue,

Mommy Knows Best

When you wake up to more wet sheets and an upset child, don't get frustrated! Only 45 percent of girls and 35 percent of boys stay dry at night before the age of three, according to an article in *Pediatrics*.

stress, and depression, all of which cause children to sleep more soundly than usual. Like youngsters suffering from primary enuresis, those with secondary enuresis are unable to wake up. The bedwetting can be expected to disappear as soon as the child is back on an even keel.

Cures for Bedwetting

Up until now, you have kept your eyes and ears open throughout the potty training process. So don't stop now. At the doctor's office, it is important to ask the right questions and listen for answers. Beware of the pediatrician who suggests your child just "isn't trying" without first doing a full medical exam (to rule out organic problems), a psychological exam (to rule out changes in the child's life that could cause increased exhaustion or stress), and a thorough family history (to investigate the possibility of an inherited problem).

Since secondary enuresis is commonly caused by stress and depression, and since punishing children causes them to feel stressed and unhappy, it is imperative that you react to bedwetting gently and with kindness. Otherwise, you'll make the situation worse rather than better.

Restricting Fluids

It makes sense just to cut down on liquids so that your little one doesn't have to go to the potty so often.

But beware of this practice! Restricting fluids in the evening is a controversial cure, which probably won't help. Normal fluid intake does not cause bedwetting. Good hydration is necessary for your child's health. When children are dehydrated their urine is more concentrated, which increases urinary urgency. It's the inability to awaken that drives enuresis.

Do eliminate liquids that irritate the bladder and increase the frequency of urination (such as caffeine), check for food allergies, and avoid lots of fluids late in the evening. To check for allergies, eliminate one type of food from your child's diet for a week and see if there is an improvement. Common allergens are milk, wheat, rye, barley, oats, eggs, soy, corn, citrus fruits, nuts, and artificial colorings or preservatives. It's the inability to awaken that drives enuresis. You can provide beverages throughout the day to your little one. Then, after dinner, only give her a drink if she asks. This should keep her from having to pass waste many times during the night.

Determine Patterns

Bedwetting treatments for children who simply cannot awaken at night aren't much help before age five or six. But it is possible to help your little one get to the bathroom at night, and get into a habit of going, by waking her and taking her there when she is still young. Bedwetting specialists recommend that parents of toddlers try to determine the time at which the accidents typically occur by conducting frequent diaper checks. Alternatively, children's beds can be outfitted with a moisture-sensitive unit that activates an alarm when urination begins. When the unit's electrical pad is moistened, a circuit closes and rings a bell or sounds a buzzer. In the past, these were very pricey items; now they are readily available through outlets that specialize in potty training products.

Keep track of wetting incidents for a week. Once you've established your child's patterns, awaken him ten to twenty minutes before he is likely to wet the bed, and take him to the bathroom to see if he can use it. Even if he never fully awakens, you may be able to avoid some accidents. Moreover, if you can consistently head them off for several months, you may be able to cure the problem by conditioning him to awaken. Exactly how this conditioning works is not understood. Rather than learning to get up at night, most children who have been successfully conditioned simply sleep through the night and stay dry without ever using the potty. If wetting resumes after they have been conditioned, they may need to be taken to the potty every night for a several nights in a row to "tune up" their brain.

Mindful Mommy

While it might be tempting to cut back on your child's fluid intake, it is important to keep your child hydrated. If he has less fluid in his body, the urine will be more concentrated. His urge to urinate will be more intense than ever before!

Medications

If your child is still wetting the bed after age five or six, there are some medications that can be helpful.

- Imipramine (also known as Tofranil) is the most commonly prescribed medication for bedwetting for older children. Although this tricyclic antidepressant can be helpful, the many difficult side effects make its advisability questionable. They include mood changes, nightmares, constipation, dry mouth, cardiac arrhythmia, drowsiness, restless legs syndrome, hypotension, confusion, tremor, dizziness, jaw cramps, and more!

- Oxybutynin chloride is a bladder antispasmodic that has been helpful to many bedwetters. Known side effects include irritability, facial flushing, and heat exhaustion during hot months. Stanford University researchers Barbara R. Sommer, William Kennedy, and Ruth O'Hara, Ph.D., note that adults who use this medication begin to show impaired memory and intellectual functioning. While the effects on children have not been studied and remain unknown, these doctors believe it is likely to have the same troubling effects.

- Desmopressin (DDAVP) is a synthetic version of a hormone the body normally produces at night to decrease urine. Even though most people urinate every few hours during the day, they are able to sleep through the night without having to get up to use the bathroom because a hormone causes the body to produce less urine. DDAVP recycles water from urine and moves it back into the bloodstream, thereby decreasing the volume of urine. Although this medication is a common treatment for chronic bedwetting, it too has difficult side effects, including nosebleeds, flushing, hypertension, and hypotension. In addition, it can interact with a wide range of medications. Bedwetting typically resumes as soon as the medication is discontinued. Still, it is a boon to older children, who may be able to use it as needed so they can attend sleepovers and summer camps.

Bedwetting Management

Be kind to your bedwetter! In an effort to protect themselves from continuing blows to their self-esteem, some youngsters adopt an I-could-care-less attitude. Parents may mistakenly conclude that they are not motivated to solve the problem or worse—are purposely wetting the bed—and react by becoming increasingly punitive. Since stress and depression cause secondary enuresis, parental negativity, shaming, and harsh punishments can cause what might have been a passing phase to become a chronic problem.

Instead, provide sympathy and reassurance that your child is still too young to awaken at night. Limit fluid intake after dinner without being overly restrictive so that your youngster remains well hydrated. Have him use the potty before bed, and take him before you turn in for the night. If that does not work, track his wetting patterns and carry him to the potty to try to head off accidents as explained previously. Put out clean pajamas if he is old enough to change into them by himself. Spread a sleeping bag on the floor so he can crawl into a clean, dry bed without awakening you.

Look for ways to lighten your workload. Use a vinyl sheet to protect the mattress and a waterproof cover over a diaper or pull-ups to contain the wetness. Even preschoolers can help remove soiled bed linen and load the washing machine (as long as they do not touch detergents and cleaning solvents!). Do not assign these tasks as a consequence or punishment! Enlisting children's help in the cleanup process gives them something positive to do about the problem and can help relieve their guilt.

Mommy Knows Best

Unfortunately, chlorine bleach and regular laundry detergents don't kill the bacterial spores that grow in urine, so the odor will reappear after linens and clothes have been washed. To get the unpleasant urine smell out of sheets and clothes, first soak them in an enzyme bleach or borax solution.

Playing with What They Produce

Touching. Smearing. Playing. Seeing youngsters handle feces can be very disgusting. Adults have been conditioned to be repelled by the odor and realize all too well the health hazards. Little ones don't yet share their views. As far as they're concerned, stool is wonderful stuff for molding and rolling and pounding.

Observing your negative reactions toward stool may help your child develop similar attitudes, which can deter him from touching it. However, rather than attempting to communicate disgust, most experts suggest a simple:

"No, we don't play with that."

Either way, carefully wash your child's hands for a minimum of twenty seconds with soap and warm water. It's important to clean under their fingernails, too, before drying their hands thoroughly.

Offer Other Gooey Goods

Increasing opportunities to play in other gooey goods such as mud and wet sand may lessen the urge to play with bodily wastes. Otherwise, sanitized versions such as Silly Putty, modeling clay, Play Dough, and finger-paints may help.

Allowing Children to Explore

Some experts point out that even a simple "No" is enough to spark determined persistence in toddlers going through the oppositional two-year-old stage. Since children are famous for sneaking into the bathroom or hiding behind a sofa to explore their bodily products, and since forbidding activities serves to increase some youngsters' interest in them, these experts say it's better to let them satisfy their curiosity in the bathroom with an adult standing by to supervise. That way, the parent can be sure none of the stool makes its way into the mouth or an eye (definitely dangerous!) and can carefully clean them afterward. This more lenient approach is believed to create positive attitudes toward bowel movements.

Feelings of embarrassment or shame can lead children to withhold stool, which can cause problems with constipation or even encopresis, so some people believe that letting children explore it will help them develop positive attitudes toward bowel movements. However, bacteria can enter the body through any skin opening, including small cuts and scrapes on the hands. There may also be benefits to teaching toddlers that human waste is simply not a plaything.

Mindful Mommy

Although some experts aren't against allowing children to play with their stool to satisfy their curiosity, this is a very risky game! Bacteria can enter their skin through a sore too small even to see!

Parents must weigh the pros and cons to decide how to handle this situation.

Explaining Chronic Soiling

Some children develop sudden problems with bowel training. After successfully using a potty chair, potty seat, or real toilet for a time, they suddenly refuse to use it. Or, they simply begin soiling for no apparent reason, and nothing their unhappy parents do seems to make a difference. But, there is in fact a reason—and lots that can be done.

A Vicious Cycle

In the absence of a medical problem, a particular chain of events can lead children to resist using a potty or toilet for bowel movements. The end result can be a full-blown case of encopresis—chronic soiling. Problems commonly begin when a child is slightly constipated. His stool is a bit harder than normal, and he associates the pain of passing it with the potty. He responds by being afraid to use the potty or even to sit on it. Alternatively, when hard stool lands in the toilet bowl, cold water splashes the child's bottom. The combination of surprise and discomfort makes him nervous about having a B.M. in the toilet again. His tension causes him to become even more constipated. When he does manage to have a B.M., the hard stools are even more painful to pass. When he manages to pass them on a toilet, they produce more splashes.

A vicious cycle develops as increasingly hard and painful bowel movements add to the child's reluctance to pass them, which increases constipation. The situation can escalate to the point that a mass of stool collects in the bowel that is too large and hard to pass through the rectum without tearing it. Liquid leaks around the hard mass. Chronic, involuntary soiling occurs, often without the child's knowledge.

Treatment for Encopresis

To break the cycle of chronic soiling, the first step is to eliminate constipation. If feeding your child more roughage, fruit, and water don't solve the problem, check with a pediatrician about mineral oil or a stool softener. Once it takes effect, it will prevent him from holding in B.M.s. The oil may take a few days to work, so if your toddler is extremely constipated, a glycerin suppository or enema may help him get started. Since mineral oil can interfere with vitamin absorption, administer it several hours after a meal or before bedtime.

Mixing the mineral oil in juice can make it more palatable. A typical starting dose of mineral oil is 1 teaspoon per ten pounds of body weight given at

Mommy Knows Best

Even a slight case of constipation can turn into a full-blown case of encopresis. Keep in mind that a child with this problem has no control. If she denies having messed her pants, she isn't lying! She just doesn't realize there was leakage night, or divided into ½ teaspoon at morning and at night. The daily dose can be increased to 3 teaspoons. If you give too much, it may leak out, leaving stains on your child's underwear. Because mineral oil increases the risk of vitamin depletion, consult your pediatrician to see if your child needs a multivitamin. If bowel movements become too frequent or watery, the dosage should immediately be reduced.

Create Positive Associations

Because many children with encopresis associate the potty with physical pain and discomfort, they may avoid the potty and become hysterical when told to use it. A return to diapers will probably be necessary. Breaking their negative associations to the potty and creating new, more positive ones may take a while and require a lot of help. Once the mineral oil takes effect and your child has been having regular soft bowel movements for ten days, rectal soreness should be completely healed. At that point, it is time to help your child tackle the potty again.

Even if your child was using the potty before problems with constipation created a setback, it may be advisable to have him practice sitting on it while wearing a diaper or pull-ups. This is especially important if he sits on a potty seat or toilet to ensure he is not splashed. If his resistance to sitting is too strong to overcome with reassurance and pep talks, offers of toys and special privileges may be necessary. At first, provide a reward for just sitting on the potty for a few seconds. To get him to sit longer, try distracting him with a quiet activity he enjoys, such as reading a book to him, playing with an Etch-A-Sketch, or reciting nursery rhymes.

Once your child sits on the potty wearing a diaper or pull-ups without a struggle for five minutes at a stretch on three consecutive days, have him sit on it bare-bottomed. Once he does that for five minutes at a time for three days, up the ante. Make rewards contingent on having a bowel movement on the potty. If he doesn't have a B.M., provide verbal praise. Tell him he can still earn the reward if he has a B.M. in the potty later. Instruct him to tell you when he needs to use it. Continue to set a timer to ensure he has a daily five-minute potty practice, but only provide a reward after he actually has a B.M. in it, which might be later in the day. You can begin reducing the mineral oil when your child's stools have remained consistently soft. Eliminate it gradually over a two-week period. Don't be surprised if the problem flares up again.

Psychological Issues

Many people, including some psychologists, believe chronic soiling is a very disturbed way to express repressed anger. Adults' aversion to soiling

Mommy Knows Best

Do what you can to keep a child who has suffered from encopresis from becoming constipated again. A minor bout of constipation can easily trigger a reoccurrence of encopresis months or even years later.

and lack of familiarity with the causes and cures has contributed to the belief that encopresis is a severe mental or behavioral disorder. Peers' reactions may be so unfavorable, sufferers can quickly develop serious psychological problems. Children with this medical problem are often depressed, socially maladjusted, and have behavior disorders. But that is the result of encopresis, not the cause. Do what you can to protect your child from psychological harm.

If caught early and treated with compassion, there is nothing to suggest encopretic children have more serious adjustment problems than those who have never experienced this problem.

Take a Time Out!
Your Little One Needs You

Everyone needs a break sometimes. Employees need coffee and lunch breaks. Football players need time-outs. Don't let potty training take over your life! Be sure to talk to your child about other things. Read books on other subjects. Praise your child for other accomplishments.

Being too preoccupied with the state of your child's bowel and bladder is likely to create the kind of stress that leads to burn-out and rebellion, depression and stress, and a wide range of physical, emotional, and psychosomatic problems. Unending concentration on potties conveys that success in this area is all that matters—and that's just not true! Your child's worth as a person is the same whether or not he is accident-free today, tomorrow, or in six months. By high school graduation, everyone manages!

If potty training is too intense for too long, you can lose your patience and objectivity. Although the diaper years can seem long indeed, someday you'll look back at this stage and be able to smile about it. You may not believe it now, but it's true. So why not start now?

Appendix A

Frequently Asked Questions

THIS BOOK CONTAINS a lot of information—and here you will find answers to many of the most common potty training questions.

What is the best age to begin potty training my daughter?

That depends on whom you ask—and when. In 1928, psychologist John Watson urged parents to hold a little pot under their infants starting in the first weeks of life. Until then, parents typically began training at age two to three months. In 1945, author and pediatrician Benjamin Spock recommended parents wait until babies could sit up by themselves. In 1961, author and pediatrician T. Berry Brazelton recommended waiting until the toddler years. More recently, he suggested it might be better to wait until around age three. Most cultures in the world still begin at age two to three months of age.

It is usually best to begin potty training before children are mobile. After that time, psychological factors become important. In general, it is best to avoid the "overly active ones" and "terrible twos." If your daughter can sit still as required (difficult for many one-year-olds), can cooperate (difficult for many two-year-olds), or is exceptionally motivated, toddler training may work well.

My son would rather have an accident than go potty when I tell him to. If I insist that he go, he throws a tantrum. What can I do?

You can't make your son take off his pants or sit much less use the potty, but you can hold a "potty practice" every hour or two, or whenever you think he needs to use it. Stay with him in the bathroom for no more than five minutes. If he has a tantrum, let it run its course. Don't talk except to remind him that he's supposed to practice sitting on the potty. Sit on the toilet and read a book (or pretend to) to show him what he's supposed to do.

The key is not to become involved in a power struggle. If he uses the potty, don't praise or reward him. Just say, "You used the potty. You can go play." If he doesn't use it, say, "Your practice is over. You can go play." If he wets himself during potty practice, just say, "You wet your pants. I need to change you." Once he understands how potty practice works, announce when it's almost time to begin. Tell him that if he uses the potty before the practice starts he will get a reward. Otherwise, have the practice session as planned.

My daughter sits on the potty, and we sing, read books, and listen to music—whatever—but nothing happens until I put her diaper back on. Then she not only goes, she goes almost immediately. But she also gets very upset about it.

Contrary to what you might think, your daughter is trying to cooperate. The problem is likely to be that she is trying too hard. As long as she is nervous, her muscles are tense. Without realizing what she is doing, she is holding in her urine and stool. When you put her back in a diaper, she finally relaxes. Her sphincter relaxes, too, so she has an accident.

Eliminate the fun and games and see if sitting quietly helps her use the potty. If not, have her go without a diaper for four or five hours every day. Try to keep her in the kitchen or another room that won't be damaged by accidents. Keep the potty nearby, but tell her not to worry about using it or having an accident. She needs pressure-free time to focus on her physical sensations so she can notice how her muscles move when she passes waste. When she figures out how her body works, she'll be able to figure out how to tense and relax the proper muscles willfully.

My son was almost potty trained, but now he won't have a B.M. in the toilet. He has a small B.M. in his pants several times a day. Sometimes he wets, too. He doesn't seem to notice or even care. I'm at a loss.

This sounds like a classic case of encopresis. When children become constipated, a mass of stool too hard to pass stays in the bowel. Softer feces make their way around the mass and leak toward the rectum. When the anal sphincter opens to release them, the urinary sphincter opens, too, so children end up wetting when they soil.

Even if your child can feel what's happening (which he probably can't), he can't control the leakage. See your pediatrician to discuss the matter. If your son is in fact encopretic, he may need a stool softener or enema until he can pass the mass, and a better diet (more vegetables, whole grains, fruit, and water) to prevent a recurrence. Once his bowel movements are back to normal, it may take a while to get him to have bowel movements in the potty again. Have him sit on it five to ten minutes around the time you expect him to have a bowel movement. Put him back in a diaper if he doesn't have one in the potty, and if he does, he can wear underpants.

Is it really possible to train infants to use the potty? How?

Yes, it is absolutely possible. This more natural training method is regaining popularity. It is more hygienic and creates stronger parent-child bonds. Parents must remain attentive in order to recognize when their infant is about to urinate or have a bowel movement. While cradling a baby, parents quickly places a pot under his bottom to "catch" the waste. They make a special "ssss" or "shshsh" sound as the infant is relieving himself. If they do this consistently, the infant develops a conditioned response. Then, whenever he recognizes the sensation of the pot on his bottom and hears the parents' special sound, he automatically pushes to relieve himself. If any waste is in his system, it will come out.

Parents can reduce or eliminate the need for diapers, and the infant doesn't have to lie in his waste, though many parents do diaper their baby at night. Infants soon begin signaling for their little pot by fussing and reaching for it when they need to eliminate, just as they signal for a bottle when they want to be fed. The biggest problem is that few mentors are available to school new mothers in the art of infant potty training. See the Resources for recommended books.

My toddler has asthma. Is it possible that he is allergic to a diapering product?

Some of the chemicals used to manufacture disposable diapers irritate the bronchial tubes and produce asthma-like symptoms in susceptible youngsters. Children don't even have to be wearing a disposable diaper to become symptomatic—simply being in the same room with one can trigger an attack. The harsh liquids used to wash cloth diapers can be a real problem, too. Be sure to put them through an extra final rinse cycle to remove chemical residues. Sometimes changing brands of disposable diapers or detergents can solve the problem. Instead of talcum powder, try cornstarch or plain flour (bake it first so it doesn't become gooey when wet). Otherwise, if you continue to suspect that a diapering product is endangering your child's health, begin potty training immediately.

My two-year-old pees in the toilet, but absolutely will not poop in it. Instead, he goes in his bedroom when he thinks I'm not looking.

This is actually a very common problem, although that doesn't make it less difficult! Potty refusals often begin during a bout of constipation. Toddlers associate the pain of passing a hard movement with the potty, and become afraid to use it again. Or, they are splashed with cold water when sitting on a potty seat on a regular toilet, and refuse to have any more bowel movements there. Many children are upset when their stool is flushed away, reacting as if part of themselves was disappearing down the drain. After wearing diapers for so long, some children are more comfortable standing or squatting during bowel movements. They have difficulty passing them when sitting down. When reprimanded for not using the potty, they take to hiding when they need to have a B.M.

Let your child wear regular underwear, and when you see signs that a bowel movement is starting, offer him a diaper. Stay close by so you can retrieve the dirty diaper afterward so he doesn't succumb to temptation and play with his B.M. Be careful he doesn't see you dispose of his diaper or its contents. Store the diaper in a lidded pail, and empty the pail when he's sleeping.

My daughter trained easily, but I'm having trouble potty training my son. I've heard boys take longer to train than girls. Is it true?

On average, boys do finish training a few months later than girls. This difference may be due to the fact that boys mature a bit more slowly. Also, little boys tend to be more active and less compliant than girls, which makes training more difficult. However, younger siblings typically train sooner because they want to mimic their big brother or sister.

Be patient with your little guy, and try not to compare your children. Each one is different, with a unique personality and rate of development. Holding one sibling to the standards of the other erodes self-esteem and can translate into sibling rivalry. What worked for your daughter may not work for your son, so check out several methods before deciding how to proceed.

My last attempt at potty training my daughter ended up being a miserable experience for both of us. Now she won't even go near the potty. Where do I go from here?

Put her back in diapers, put the potty away, and give her a month to forget. Then, start reintroducing the potty very gradually. Put it in her play area so she can see it for a few days. Then invite her to sit on it fully clothed while you read her a story. Have her accompany you to the bathroom or leave the door open so she can watch you use the toilet. Ask her to hand you toilet paper and help you flush. A few days later, put her potty in the bathroom and suggest she feed a doll-that-wets a bottle. Then suggest she have the doll use the potty while you use the toilet. Next, suggest she sit on the potty chair in the bathroom while you read her a story. After a few days of story reading, see if she will sit on her potty with nothing on her bottom. Tell her she is "just like Mama." Thereafter, see if you can get her to sit on the potty once a day without anything on her bottom, timing it so she might use it, and praising her if she succeeds. Whatever you do, avoid chastising her for accidents. Instead, try a reward system.

Does the way toddlers are potty trained form their personalities?

No. It is a myth the parents' approach to potty training affects personality! Children's personalities dictate how easy or difficult they are to potty train. Easy-going youngsters with regular systems who adapt well to change are usually easiest to train. Shy youngsters are often more fearful of the potty at the outset and have bigger setbacks if something scares them during training. Insecure youngsters can become overwhelmed if the pace of potty training is too fast, and they are more inclined to give up when they are criticized for accidents. More active children have a harder time sitting still, which can make them more difficult to train. But they may enjoy running to the potty and climbing onto a potty seat. Parents have a harder time helping an irregular child get to the potty at the right time, which makes it harder to teach them.

Certainly, abusing children during potty training warps their personality development, and shaming and humiliating them erodes their self-esteem. Harsh criticism can upset an overly sensitive tyke enough to cause Post Traumatic Stress Syndrome, a serious emotional disorder. Barring something so drastic, potty training doesn't have much, if anything to do with personality development. Parents have less of a hand in molding their children than people generally think!

What rewards work best for toddlers?

It really depends on the toddler! A smile and approving nod is all the reward many youngsters need. However, during the oppositional two-year-old stage, children are often driven to do the opposite of whatever they think that their parents want them to do, so parental praise may backfire. A spray of perfume and the statement, "You smell as pretty as a flower now that you used the potty instead of wetting your diapers" delights little boys as well as little girls. Stickers and the chance to wear real underwear are popular rewards. Nevertheless, some toddlers lose interest once the novelty wears off. The chance to earn a Hot Wheel toy has induced lots of toddler boys to drop everything and run to the potty time and again. The opportunity to do something special such as paint or blow bubbles works for many toddlers. To be effective, rewards must be given immediately after a potty success. Lots of parents find that an M&M, animal cracker, or piece of sweetened cereal works better than anything else. Remember that rewards can be used to reinforce any "success," including just sitting on the potty.

My son hasn't had an accident during the day for six months, but he still wets the bed at night. Is this normal?

Although there are no hard and fast rules, children typically start staying dry at night at about the same time they start using the potty regularly during the day. Children with a relative who wet the bed as a youngster are at greater risk for bedwetting. More boys wet the bed than girls. Anxiety and depression can cause bouts of bedwetting. Eventually, most children simply outgrow it.

Treatments aren't available until age five, so about the only solution is to try to cut down on the number of accidents by limiting fluids in the evening and taking your son to the potty during the night. Put your child to bed in a diaper and use a waterproof pad to protect the mattress. If you can determine when the wetting usually happens and carry him to the potty before then, you may prevent it. After being taken regularly during the night for a time, some children stop bedwetting.

Whatever you do, don't get angry! Bedwetting isn't something children can control. Since anxiety and depression can also cause bedwetting, punishments can make things worse.

My thirty-month-old is so defiant, I've been dreading trying to potty train him. My mother has offered to give it a try. I'm wondering if I should let her.

Because toddlers are trying to establish a separate identity, they usually save their worst behavior for the people they are closest to. Your son might in fact respond better to someone with whom he has a less intense relationship, assuming that it is a good one. Toddlers are often "trained" to use the potty by day care friends and older siblings.

Talk to your mother first to be sure you are comfortable with the methods she plans to use. You must be able to support her efforts by using the same methods in your home.

Potty training is stressful because children are excited, are learning so many new things at once, and must really concentrate. Unless your youngster is accustomed to being with his grandmother for extended periods, a bout of homesickness could end up making it harder for him to give potty training his all.

Additional Resources

As you prepare for training your child—or continue your ongoing efforts—you'll find a variety of resources for adults and children. Parenting books, videos, and Web sites are all excellent sources of information. Remember, however, that if you have concerns regarding your child's health or well being, you should discuss the matter with your child's pediatrician.

Children's Books

Sanschagrin, Joceline and Helene Desputeaux. *Caillou-Potty Time* (Chouette Publishing, 2000). If your toddler's PBS hero can do it, so can your toddler.

Mack, Allison. *Dry All Night* (Little, Brown, & Company, 1989). This book is for parents (Part 1) and for older children who can read (Part 2). It's definitely worth a look-see if bedwetting is hampering your youngster's social life.

Gomi, Taro and Amanda Mayer Stinchecum. *Everybody Poops* (Kane/Miller Publisher, 1993). This book explains elimination in terms little ones can understand.

Worth, Bonnie and David Prebenna (Illustrator). *I Can Go Potty* (Bonnie Worth, 1999). If Kermit can do it, so can your child.

Cole, Joanna and Maxie Chambliss. *My Big Boy Potty and My Big Girl Potty.* (HarperCollins Juvenile Books, 2000). The text reassures little ones that practice makes perfect and gives the impression that anyone can accomplish this feat.

Frankel, Alona. *Once Upon a Potty* (HarperCollins Juvenile Books, 1999). Available in boy and girl formats and packaged with a doll, this book can be used to introduce babies and toddlers to a new potty, but even three-year-olds find the messages about accidents reassuring.

Capucilli, Alissa S. and Dorothy Stott (Illustrator). *The Potty Book for Boys* (Barrons Educational Series, 2000). A rhyming picture book.

Lewison, Wendy. *The Princess and the Potty* (Aladdin Paperbacks, 1998). The princess breaks down and uses the potty so as not to wet her darling pantaloons.

McGrath, Bob and Shelley Dieterichs (Illustrator). *Uh Oh! Gotta Go!* (Barrons Juveniles, 1996). Yet another good one.

Borgardt, Marianne and Maxie Chambliss (Illustrator). *What Do You Do with a Potty?: An Important Pop-up Book* (Golden Books, 1994). Your child can pull, lift, and learn.

Murkoff, Heidi and Laura Rader (Illustrator). *What to Expect When You Use the Potty* (HarperCollins Juvenile Books, 2000). Another good one to add to your child's collection.

Kriegman, Janelle, Mitchell Kriegman, and Kathryn Mitter (Illustrator). *When You've Got to Go!* (Bear in the Big Blue House) (Simon Spotlight, 2000). This one is sure to build enthusiasm for potty training. The book comes packaged with the video, Bear in the Big Blue House—Potty Time with Bear (1997) by Mitchell Kriegman and Richard A. Fernandes, Directors.

Cole, Joanna, with photos by Margaret Miller. *Your New Potty* (Morrow Junior Books, 1989). The introduction contains guidelines for parents.

Potty Training Books for Parents

Azrin, Nathan H. and Richard M. Foxx. *Toilet Training in a Day* (Pocket Books, 1974). A step-by-step guide to putting children age two and over on the fast track to speed learning.

Boucke, Laurie. *Infant Potty Training* (White-Boucke Publishing, 2002). If you don't believe infant potty training is the gentler, more natural way before you read this comprehensive tome on the subject, you will afterwards!

Faull, Jan. *Mommy I Have to Go Potty: A Parent's Guide to Toilet Training* (Parenting Press, 1996). A potties-without-pressure approach for older toddlers who are self-motivated.

Schaefer, Charles E. and Theresa Foy DiGeronimo. *Toilet Training without Tears* (Signet Penguin Group, 1997). Learn to set loving limits, and read about the special techniques for training children with developmental delays.

Sonna, Linda. *Early-Start Potty Training* (McGraw Hill, 2005). Instructions for potty training infants, babies, young toddlers, as well as older children who are having problems progressing.

VanPelt, Katie. *Potty Training Your Baby* (Avery Publishing Group, 1996). Start early on, after youngsters can sit up and long before the terribly trying twos begin, and potty training is likely to be much easier.

Technical Journal Articles

"Diagnosis and Treatment for Children Who Cannot Control Urination." Max Maizels, Kevin Gandhi, Barbara Keating, and Diane Rosenblum. *Current Problems in Pediatrics*, November/December, 1993 (pages 402–450). If your child's pediatrician isn't knowledgeable about all of the organic problems and treatments for uncontrolled wetting—and many are not—this article can fill them in.

Professional Help

Potty training S.O.S. Telephone consultations. *www.DrSonna.org*

National Enuresis Society (NES). A not-for-profit organization of doctors, medical personnel, and other persons dedicated to building greater awareness and understanding of enuresis. (Now part of the National Kidney Foundation.) *www.kidney.org*

National Kidney Foundation (NKF). Supports children with bedwetting and their families, and provides information to professionals. Call 1-888-WAKE-DRY, or see *www.bedwetting-nkfonline.org*.

Try for Dry. Get products for help diagnosing and treating bedwetting from the company that trains the docs! Call (773) 989-1960, see *www.tryfordry.com*, or e-mail info@tryfordry.com.

Online Resources

www.DrSonna.org. Free potty training chart and stickers; help from the author.

www.babyminestore.com. Baby-friendly diapers, diaper covers, training pants, potty seats, and more. Phone (623) 974-4457 for a catalog.

www.babyparenting.about.com. Potty training tips and the chance to network with other online parents are a click away.

www.parents-choice.org. Books, toys, videos, and software that other parents have given a thumbs-up.

www.pottytrainingsolutions.com. The one-stop Web site for training products, books, tapes, even homeopathic remedies. Phone (480) 883-9765 for a catalog.

www.tnpc.com. Before you buy a potty chair, check the recommendations and recalls at the National Parenting Center's Seal of Approval Web site.

General Parenting Books

Sonna, Linda. *The Everything® Toddler Book* (Adams Media, 2002).

Brazelton, T. Berry. *Touchpoints, The Essential Reference: Your Child's Emotional and Behavioral Development* (Addison-Wesley Publishing Company, 1992).

Eisenberg, Arlene, Sandee E. Hathaway, and Heidi E. Murkoff. *What to Expect the Toddler Years* (Workman Publishing, 1996).

Index

Help Is on the Way
from Adams Media!

(Spiral-bound trade paperback, $12.95)

ISBN 10: 1-59869-332-8

ISBN 13: 978-1-59869-332-4

ISBN 10: 1-59869-333-6

ISBN 13: 978-1-59869-333-1

ISBN 10: 1-59869-334-4

ISBN 13: 978-1-59869-334-8

ISBN 10: 1-59869-331-X

ISBN 13: 978-1-59869-331-7

Available wherever books are sold.

Or call us at 1-800-258-0929 or visit us at www.adamsmedia.com.